From Bedlam to Bethlehem

Finding Christmas in Chaos

J. William Harris

SMYTH & HELWYS
PUBLISHING, INC.

Macon, Georgia

ISBN 1-57312-016-2

From Bedlam to Bethlehem
Finding Christmas in Chaos
J. William Harris

Copyright ©1995
Smyth & Helwys Publishing, Inc.®
6316 Peake Road
Macon, Georgia 31210-3960
1-800-568-1248

Library of Congress Cataloging-in-Publication Data

Harris, J. William.
    From bedlam to Bethlehem
        vii + 145pp.   6" x 9" (15 x 23 cm.)
    ISBN 1-57312-016-2
    1. Advent–Meditations. 2. Devotional calendars.
BV40.H356 1995   95–17304
242'.33–dc20   CIP

May the love, hope, peace, and joy of the Christ child be yours.

Bill Harris

From Bedlam
to Bethlehem

Finding Christmas in Chaos

To our children
Who keep alive the wonder of Christmas

Julianne
Heather
Jamie

Contents

The Fourth Week of Advent
DRAMATIS PERSONAE

The Enduring Message of Christmas

Preface

Several years ago at Christmas, a friend wrote an article in his church newsletter about the origin of the word "bedlam." This term for confusion and disintegration, he noted, derived from "Bethlehem," the birthplace of our Lord. How intriguing that a word associated with beauty and wonder should become a word descriptive of chaos!

Bethlehem, however, remains intact. Christ has come and continues to come. Gradually his work in our lives and in the world reverses the processes that we set in motion. Jesus Christ is leading us back to Bethlehem. Christmas celebrates that work, God's gracious work of salvation and restoration. It symbolizes what God has done and continues to do. The distortion of Christmas through busyness and commercialization can lead us to bedlam; the appreciation of Christmas guides us to Bethlehem.

Whether we move toward Bethlehem or bedlam depends in large part on the preparation we make as Christmas approaches. The church has understood the need for preparation of the heart. The Advent season addresses that need. Beginning on the Sunday nearest 30 November, the season can provide a period as long as four full weeks. Advent invites meditation on the past, present, and future of the Christ event. It explores the prophetic anticipation of the messiah, the birth narratives, and the implications of the coming of Christ for individual life and for history.

I offer these readings for the Advent season with the hope that they can help bring enrichment to a season that is losing significance for many Christians and with the prayer that they can enhance the celebration of Christmas among those who seek to move from bedlam to Bethlehem.

My appreciation I express freely and joyfully to the church family at First Baptist Church in Greenwood, South Carolina. This church knows how to celebrate Christmas. From it I have learned much, and through it I have experienced much. Some of my most cherished moments of worship have come in the midnight service conducted here on Christmas Eve. The annual family night at Christmas, the Advent observances, the "spare no pains" approach to proclaiming and sharing the Christ of Christmas have made the season for me a time of growth. Special thanks to the church secretaries/ministers—Grace Burton, Lois Grice, Nell Morton, and Joyce Williams—who helped with the typing of the manuscript and patiently guided me into the use of a word processor.

My enduring gratitude I give to Linda, whose love and encouragement are my constant motivation.

Bill Harris
Greenwood, South Carolina

The First
Week of Advent

The Need for Preparation

Day One
God's Decision About Life

But when the fullness of time had come, God sent his Son, born of woman, born under the law, in order to redeem those who were under the law, so that we might receive adoption as children.

–(Gal 4:4-5)

When God called Abraham into a covenant relationship, initiating what we call "holy history," God gave a sign of divine faithfulness in the birth of Isaac. When God was ready to deliver the Israelites from Egyptian bondage and to establish them as a nation, God began to act with the birth of Moses. Later when Israel came to the third great period of its history, the creation of the monarchy, Samuel was born.

Each account of these sweeping Old Testament events was preceded by a birth narrative. Ancient Hebrew writers saw each successive era beginning with the birth of a child. Therefore, we should not be surprised that the New Testament begins with the story of a birth. We hail the announcement of the angel, "To you is born this day in the city of David a Savior, who is the Messiah, the Lord" (Luke 2:11), as God's decision about life, a pivotal turn in God's relationship with humanity.

On this planet today four babies are born every second. Birth and death alike are common occurrences, and, until they touch us directly as in the death of a loved one or the birth of our own child or grandchild, we take them pretty much for granted. That's our loss! Each birth adds so much to life, and each death takes so much away.

Whatever we do, we cannot afford to be indifferent about the birth we celebrate at Christmas. The birth of Jesus Christ affects the lives of us all in a direct way. By birth into a human family, Jesus Christ has literally been born into the family of each of us. No family nor life is too humble for him. In fact, circumstances surrounding the birth of Christ hardly signaled the beginning of a new age. Into a rough-and-tumble world of struggle, suffering, and need Jesus came—which says much concerning God's decision about life. The idea that the child was born homeless, that his first admirer was a shepherd with an unshaven face and toothless smile, tells us that he is willing to be born even today into the life and circumstances of anyone. All the people of the world, even those who feel insignificant and forgotten, can gather around the manger and say that the baby lying there belongs to them.

If anyone should doubt this sign, he/she must look at the life of the man who this baby grew to be. In his ministry Jesus never abandoned the lowliness and simplicity of his birth. He called his followers from among fishermen and tax collectors. He visited ordinary homes, such as that of Mary, Martha, and Lazarus in Bethany. He dealt with people in their ordinary pursuits. To convey his message, he told simple stories drawn from his observation of everyday life. God's concern for individuals, Jesus said, is like the care of a shepherd for one lost sheep; the word is sown in the way a sower casts the seed. God's acceptance is like that of a father for a lost son.

We put forth our theories about the meaning of the Incarnation and work out our theological systems, but we can say little that will improve on what the presence of the Christ child says: that God has come to be with us and will stay with us! But that's not all. God's decision about human life is not simply to be a part of it, but to change it. The child whose birth we prepare to celebrate became the man who said, "I came that they may have life, and have it abundantly" (John 10:10). Abundant life calls for more than just a presence; it requires transformation. And so, Christ comes to us and begins his work in us.

Christ deals with dark, ugly things such as sin and guilt. He gets to our fears and anxieties and encourages us to trust. He destroys the barriers that limit our vision and teaches us to look for things that truly matter. He directs us to our responsibilities toward others. We learn what it means to forgive, to be reconciled, to discover a new level of living, a level of life like his life. As we begin to take on Christ-likeness, as we begin to feel and show the love revealed by God in Christ, we begin to understand something concerning God's decision about life. The Christ comes to be with us; he stays to change us.

Once in a meeting with a group of Quakers, Helen Keller sat in silence with the other worshipers. Silence, of course, was nothing new or unusual for her; she had been unable to hear or see since she was nineteen months-old. At the appropriate time, she rose to speak. She thanked the Friends for their vivid interpretation of love and brotherhood. Then, with extraordinary effect, she described her own liberation.

When she was a little girl, Helen Keller said, she was shut up in utter darkness. When she was age seven, Helen was placed in the hands of Miss Anna Sullivan, who had, for a time, been blind. With patience and tenderness, Miss Sullivan brought her into contact with the world that was up to then beyond her reach. She interpreted the world to Helen and opened within her undreamed-of capabilities for participation in that new world of life and thought. Even with closed eyes Helen Keller learned to see a world of beauty, hope, and possibility.

This story, so familiar and so heart-warming, reflects in a partial, limited way what Christ does in us. He enters our world, takes upon himself our darkness, and places himself under our burden. In doing so, he opens our blind eyes to the light of God's glory, unseals our deaf ears to the word of God's truth, and brings us into a life of greater depth and meaning than we ever imagined.

The birth of the Christ child is God's decision that human life should not only continue but become like God's life. Toward that end we begin the journey into a season of preparation.

Day Two
"Prepare the Way of the Lord"

The word of God came to John son of Zechariah in the wilderness. He went into all the region around the Jordan, proclaiming a baptism of repentance for the forgiveness of sins, as it is written in the book of the words of the prophet Isaiah, "The voice of one crying out in the wilderness: 'Prepare the way of the LORD, make his paths straight. Every valley shall be filled, and every mountain and hill shall be made low, and the crooked shall be made straight, and the rough ways made smooth; and all flesh shall see the salvation of God.' "

—(Luke 3:2b-6)

It takes a while to "get into" Christmas. The Christmas spirit is not an automatic response to a date on the calendar. For many persons the approach of Christmas represents something of a burden. There seems to be so much to do: buying gifts, decorating the house, planning extra activities, meeting additional responsibilities. We tend to feel very uneasy around the end of November, because we feel unprepared for something very important.

The outward trappings of Christmas pose only one level of unreadiness. There is also the matter of preparing the spirit to experience anew and to proclaim again the most wonderful event in human history—the Incarnation, the coming of the Christ. We are less than honest if we do not confess a profound sense of need at that point.

Advent addresses these feelings of unpreparedness. It calls us to ready the mind and the heart to celebrate the birth of Jesus Christ 2,000 years ago and to ponder the meaning of his living presence in our world today. Since the sixth century the Christian church has observed the Advent season as a time of anticipation, penitence, solemnity, joy, and expectancy. These very things are reflected in the message of John the Baptist, the forerunner and witness, the one who came to prepare the way for the ministry of Jesus. John's preaching depicted precisely what we seek to derive from the spirit of Advent.

From Bedlam to Bethlehem

First was the blunt imperative: "Prepare the way of the LORD." John was speaking to a diverse group of people. He addressed the poor, the downtrodden, and the oppressed—persons for whom hope had faded. He addressed religious and political leaders, those who felt that hope for their world rested in their own efforts. He addressed persons who accepted their designation as common sinners, those who questioned the possibility of hope. To them all John announced that God was ready to act in a unique way, and within them all he sought to arouse the hope of God's visitation among humanity. Into a world of darkness and despair, a light was coming. Hope, long dormant and distorted, was about to be fulfilled. Let hearts be prepared for God's mighty work, John preached.

Preparation is vital. We begin Advent by dusting off our hopes. We allow our spirits to respond to the winsome strains of the ancient song:

> O come, O come, Emmanuel
> And ransom captive Israel,
> That mourns in lonely exile here
> Until the Son of God appear.
> Rejoice! Rejoice!
> Emmanuel shall come to thee, O Israel.[1]

We dare to believe the truth contained in that beautiful term "Emmanuel" —God with us.

The call of Advent to a renewal of hope and expectancy is a welcome summons. Most of the time we fret with our problems and worry about the dire predictions we hear concerning the course of life. We lose sight of our belief that God is still at work in our world. The world of beauty, order, and peace described by the Old Testament prophets is far from being a reality. The kingdom of God proclaimed by our Lord seems far removed from life as we know it. As we move into the season of Advent, however, we reaffirm that God's designs for human life have not been discarded and that the God who came in Jesus Christ still is coming to redeem and restore.

6

Christians should be an expectant people, looking forward to the way of the Lord. Only as we live in hope do we live at all. Living with anticipation instead of resignation and dread gives us the kind of attitude that enables us to respond to new opportunities. We believe that God has something for us to do in the redemptive process, and we remain constantly on the lookout for it.

John's second imperative took up the matter of penitence: "Make his paths straight." Those in his congregation by the Jordan River clearly understood what he meant. In ancient times when a king set out to visit his subjects, servants went before him to prepare the way. They repaired roads, removed obstacles, and provided resting places. John saw himself as the courier of the king of kings. In essence, he said, "Mend not your roads, but your hearts."

The Christ comes not simply to bless but also to judge, not simply to build up but also to tear down. Do you remember what the aged Simeon told Mary in the temple? Lifting the child from his mother's arms, he said,

> This child is destined for the fall and the rising of many in Israel, and to be a sign that will be opposed so that the inner thoughts of many will be revealed—and a sword will pierce your own soul too.
> —(Luke 2:34-35)

The coming of Christ brings judgment for each of us. By his truth we measure our values and priorities. To his example we compare our selfishness and pretense. With his love we contrast our indifference and exclusiveness. We cannot escape from the judgment that the light of Christ has brought into the world: "The crooked shall be made straight, and the rough places plain."

Even if we fail to see and understand, the message goes forth. John concluded his message with the assertion: "All flesh shall see the salvation of God." We proclaim that God has acted, that the Word has become flesh. No longer are we merely encouraged with promises. God has already come in a decisive way.

Constantly the preacher or the teacher searches for new or different ways to describe the miracle of the Incarnation. Our telling

7

of the story seems repetitious. When we wrestle with that problem, we need to realize that the story really requires no embellishment. The Gospel writers told it with stark simplicity: God has become man, that man might be reclaimed by God. God has experienced our feelings and frustrations, felt our hurts and suffered with us in our sins; God has come to know our sharp sting of pain and has identified with us; God has made us God's own and will never leave us. That message cannot be improved. It simply needs to be proclaimed until all who hurt in any way find healing.

Christ's coming is a message of change and new possibilities. Elizabeth Barrett Browning once wrote to her beloved husband Robert: "The face of all the world is changed, I think, since first I heard the footsteps of thy soul." In an infinitely larger dimension, this is the content of our proclamation. The coming of Christ means that everything has been changed.

The Incarnation, the coming of God into human life and history, means that the one who created continues to create, that the one who reigned continues to reign. William Temple reminded us that this authentic note of the gospel ought to characterize the message the church takes to the world. Temple said,

> While we deliberate, God reigns; when we decide wisely, He reigns; when we decide foolishly, He reigns; when we serve humbly and loyally, He reigns; when we rebel and seek to withhold our service, He reigns—the Alpha and Omega, which is, and which was, and which is to come, the Almighty.[2]

Anyone who doubts the activity of God and the ultimate triumph of God's kingdom needs to hear the proclamation of this truth of Advent. The apostles understood this concept, and their cry and prayer was, "Come, Lord Jesus." They longed for the revelation voiced by John, that "all flesh see the salvation of God." So do true believers today. We prepare for it; we repent that we might receive it; we share it. If this is our attitude, we participate in the life Christ came to bring. What we say about our faith takes form in our personality. It directs our thoughts and finds expression in our actions.

We learn to appreciate the truth of the Incarnation only as we participate with Christ in his work, as we come to know him personally and intimately. Without that personal relationship and commitment to his goals, we will not likely be moved by the retelling of the story of Christmas. Truth is gained by experience.

John Steinbeck holds a place among the most widely read and influential American novelists of the twentieth century. Although he went to Stanford off and on for five years, Steinbeck never received his degree. He was too busy to focus on that. While he was a student, he was also a road worker, a rancher, a dockhand, and a farmer. He traveled across the country. He involved himself in the lives of people who later became the subjects for his writing. He prepared himself for writing *The Grapes of Wrath* by following migrants from Oklahoma to California, by living with them and coming to identify with their struggles and heartaches. He learned the truths he explored in his stories by roaming over and becoming one with a rough and demanding terrain.

In a similar manner we learn of Christ. Our best knowledge of him comes not from books and second-hand accounts, not even in the celebration of a religious season, but from being with him and letting him come fully into our lives.

Day Three
If Christ Had Not Come

Get you up to a high mountain, O Zion, herald of good tidings; lift up your voice with strength, O Jerusalem, herald of good tidings, lift it up, do not fear; say to the cities of Judah, "Here is your God!" See, the LORD God comes with might, and his arm rules for him; his reward is with him, and his recompense before him. He will feed his flock like a shepherd; he will gather the lambs in his arms, and carry them in his bosom, and gently lead the mother sheep.

—(Isa 40:9-11)

By early December the services and activities have been planned. The decorations are going up. Rehearsals for seasonal events are underway. The externals are taking shape. Churches and individuals are preparing to celebrate the coming of Jesus Christ, our Savior and Lord. Sometimes perhaps we take this process for granted. We go about it routinely. It's as if we know what will happen or how the story ends and therefore take the whole thing rather casually, so maybe we should begin the Advent season from a different perspective. Usually the theme is the coming of light into darkness or the meaning of the Christ event. Let's stretch our minds a little and look at something less predictable. What if Jesus Christ had not come? What would life and faith be like had God not sent Jesus into the world?

For many people, Jesus Christ has not come. Millions have never heard his name. Others have heard the name of Jesus Christ but do not recognize him as determinative for life and history. The supposed intellectual approach to reality acknowledges the possibility of some supreme being but rejects the notion of a God who has revealed God's self in human form. This is a projection of human wishing, the argument goes. Then some people take no position. They neither affirm nor deny the coming and impact of Christ. They simply ignore him. For those folks also, Jesus Christ has not come.

How do you describe a world without Christ? What would it be like to have a life with no connection to or relationship with Christ? When we try to imagine such a situation, several issues come to mind.

First, if Christ had not come, we would have no personal knowledge of God. We believe that Jesus Christ is God incarnate, or God in human flesh. That God has come to be one of us means that God understands us and identifies with us, and that God's love is such that God forms with us an indissoluble bond. Take that away and we are left with a very unclear view of God. Take that away and God seems removed and distant. Terms such as Supreme Being and First Cause have little meaning. They give rise to fear instead of love, arouse superstition instead of reverence, and lead to appeasement rather than worship.

If Christ had not come, we could speak of the existence of God, but we would not perceive the overwhelming significance of God. If we had a relationship with God at all, it would be a relationship of law and duty, not a relationship of love. We would have to remove the heart from our faith. Our faith would be a religion of form; we would leave its upkeep to priests. It would not be a living, growing dynamic in life.

Second, if Christ had not come, we would be left with a terrible sense of loneliness. This would be a cold, hard universe indeed. How would we ever cope with pain, loss, or death? If Christ had not come, there would be no one to help us when we face a personal challenge, no one to express and assure us of forgiveness when we know we have committed a wrong, no one to renew our strength when we are weary, no one to tell us that when this life is over, it is not really over. Take away a personal savior, and this world is an extremely lonely place. We have persons who try to empathize with us, but their efforts have limits.

A seminary student once told about a course in urban studies that took him out among the street people in a large city. He and other class members put on old clothes and worn-out shoes and mingled for two days with the homeless. They stood in line for food at a soup kitchen. They joined in the search for a warm place to sleep. They listened to the stories of failure and tragedy. After two days the experience for the seminarians ended. They left the streets, showered, put on clean clothes, and returned to a life of comfort.

People around us can enter our situation just so much. If we do not have one who stays, who understands completely, who will not leave us or forsake us, what do we have? Loneliness settles in quickly.

Third, if Christ had not come, we would lack a purpose for living. Of all creatures, the human alone asks why. Perhaps that question makes us human. We are given minds, abilities, opportunities, and challenges. We work, achieve, and grow. Yet, we also lose all our gifts. We face pain and death. Without some sense of purpose in this life, we would at best hesitate to give ourselves in service and at worst be driven to insanity. We must have purpose.

To take life seriously is to look for purpose. Professor Arnold Toynbee, at the end of ten volumes on human civilizations, said: "The entire story of man on earth has no meaning at all except a religious meaning. There is no hope except in the vast increase of spiritual insight." As believers we affirm that Christ is our purpose, that we live in his love, grow in his truth, and commit our present and future to his work of redemption and reconciliation. If Christ had not come, what could we say about purpose?

Fourth, if Christ had not come, there would be no moral guidelines for living. Remove from your consciousness the call to love God and love one's neighbor, take away from your mind Christian ethical concerns, and what do you have? You would have moral chaos. Promises would have no meaning. Relationships would have no value. Crime, corruption, and cruelty to others would pass without notice. No one would be outraged, no one would work to overcome injustice, no one would take the side of the victim. The world would be a frightening place in which to live.

No personal understanding of God, a sense of loneliness, a lack of purpose, moral and ethical relativity—such things depict the way life would be had Christ not come. As we speculate on such a situation, it occurs to us that this is not speculation to most people; it is a description of life as it is. When you hear the reports of abuse and suffering, when you consider the values that seem to guide our society, when you survey the approaches people take to evade reality and try to find some relief from a burdensome existence, you get the sinking feeling that for many Christ really has not come. We ask ourselves what his coming really means for us. Is it simply a casual affirmation, or is it the basic truth of life? The coming of Christ is the central event of history. It is the key to understanding all things. It is the first and basic fact. Take that away, and we have nothing.

Colombian author Gabriel Garcia Marquez has a story about a village where people were afflicted with a strange plague of forgetfulness, a kind of contagious amnesia. Starting with the oldest inhabitants and working its way through the population, the plague caused people to forget the names of even the most common everyday objects. One young man, while still unaffected, saw what was happening. He sought to limit the damage by putting labels on everything: "This is a window." "This is a cow, it has to be milked every morning." At the entrance to the town, on the main road, he put up two large signs. One read: "The name of our village is Macondo." The other one, in much larger letters, read, "God exists!"

God exists! God has made God's self known in Jesus Christ. That is the first, the last, the basic fact of history. We could possibly live in this world, even live in our society, and never know that God exists or that Christ has come. Our message is that Christ has come and that he is coming. Let us put that truth over our community and across our hearts.

Day Four
What Will You Get
from Christmas?

In the beginning was the Word, and the Word was with God, and the Word was God. He was in the beginning with God. All things came into being through him, and without him not one thing came into being. What has come into being in him was life, and the life was the light of all people. The light shines in the darkness, and the darkness did not overcome it.

—(John 1:1-5)

At Christmastime the mind is flooded with vivid memories from childhood. I distinctly remember the question that my friends and I used to ask each other as the days before Christmas slowly dragged by: What are you going to get for Christmas? Of course, if you asked someone else that question, you were supposed to have your own turn to recite the list of things you wanted or expected to receive. Somehow, repeating the list served to intensify the anticipation of Christmas. Often our desires were unrealistic and as a result were not fulfilled, but we always knew what we wanted.

I have a similar question: What are you going to get from Christmas? What will you be left with when the day and the season are over? I ask this question because I believe that ultimately we discover what we seek and that we will derive from something like Christmas that which we most sincerely desire.

We make extensive preparations for Christmas. We arrange our schedules to include as many activities as possible, decorate homes and offices and stores, shop for gifts, and yes, we go to church. What comes of all this?

Contrary to what the television specials and the brightly colored cards would lead us to believe, not everyone experiences tranquility and happiness. Loneliness and depression are more common at this time of year than we like to admit. Many persons feel left out; they have no one with whom to celebrate. Others feel a sense of emptiness. They ask why people make such a fuss over an event that seems only to arouse hopes that do not materialize.

Many people end the season only with fatigue and perhaps the dread of the bills for purchases through which they thought they could buy Christmas joy.

Christmas is an extremely busy time, to be sure, but we should get more from it than exhaustion. We have the wonderful opportunity for personal renewal. We can gain a fresh appreciation for the beauty and wonder of the love God revealed in the birth of Jesus Christ. We can broaden our faith and deepen our commitment to the Christ whose presence is as real today as it was on that holy night in Bethlehem.

These blessings to the human spirit do not come automatically, however. They come to the heart that is ready to receive them. Just as there is an art to giving, there is an art to receiving. We get from Christmas what we are able to receive.

The prologue to John's Gospel gives a sweeping description of what the coming of Christ means to our world and our lives. John did not give a narrative of Jesus' birth; we have that in the accounts of Matthew and Luke. Instead, John attempted to interpret the event. He wanted to convey the uniqueness of God's gift of God's self in Jesus Christ and sought to explain the difference that the coming of Christ makes in the scheme of things. John saw the incarnation of God in Christ as something altogether new and wonderful. If we can come to a deeper understanding of this concept, we will receive some things of great value from Christmas.

First, we can discover a sense of wonder toward God's gift of God's self. "In the beginning was the Word, and the Word was with God, and the Word was God . . . And the Word became flesh and lived among us." Perhaps this verse seems to be an odd way of stating the truth of Christmas, but, in fact, these lines touch the heart of the matter. In the thought of John's day, Word or *Logos* was an important concept. The Greek thinkers discussed the *Logos* as the primary philosophical principle. They identified the *Logos* as the basis for order and continuity in the world, the mind of God after which people sought but found incomprehensible. Jewish theologians understood the Logos to be the sovereign energy through which God carried out God's purpose in the affairs of men and women. They believed that the *Logos* was identical to God's law and wisdom.

John deliberately used the terminology of his day to describe the wonder of the Incarnation. He said that the divine power, the rational principle, the *Logos*, whatever one would call ultimate truth, has been fully revealed in Jesus Christ. No longer is God the object of a human search; God has uncovered the divine self and has made it known in a person. Thus, we can speak of the humanity of God and of God's identification with our situation.

What does this mean for us? It means that God is not the subject of conjecture; God is not unknowable. Who is God, and what is God like? We find the answers to these questions, not from our own search, but from our relationship with Jesus. It also means that God is with us, active in our lives and concerned with our affairs. When we speak of God's presence and activity in the world, we are not talking about a vague awareness or an occasional feeling; we are talking about a present reality. When we describe our faith, we do not talk in terms of religious ideas and doctrines; we describe an experience.

Certainly, the mysterious element has not been completely removed. Far from it! We are surrounded by mystery. We cannot say how or why the event occurred as it did. The truth of it all remains awe-inspiring. Have we become so preoccupied that we are not touched by this miracle? Have we become so disinclined to serious thought that we are content with the externals of Christmas? Then a renewal of wonder is one thing we need to get from this Christmas.

Second, we could get from Christmas a new appreciation of the light that has entered our world. In his gospel and letters John makes much of the contrast between light and darkness, between what is true and what is false. Women and men hunger for the light. We can feel the anticipation of Isaiah who wrote, "The people who walked in darkness have seen a great light; those who lived in a land of deep darkness—on them light has shined" (9:2). John responds to this longing by saying, "The true light, which enlightens everyone, was coming into the world."

To say that this "light shines in the darkness" means that Christmas is the story of God's radical invasion into the real world in which we live all year long. The light comes to judge the world, to bring truth and justice into every dark corner. It exposes everything that is false. It points to areas of need, poverty and hunger, hatred and jealousy. The light gives direction to God's people for their life in the world, and it gives hope to the yearning that things can be different. Thus, we say that "the darkness did not overcome it."

The darkness cannot overcome the light, but indifference among the children of light can leave it dim. In hearts that have grown hard and complacent, the light loses its vitality. Perhaps Christmas reminds us in many ways of our failure to tend the light we have received. Do you ever hear someone say, "I wish the spirit of Christmas could last all year"? That frequent comment is a reflection on our attitudes. It indicates that the attitude of giving and kindness so freely demonstrated at this time of year is lacking at other times. The light is dim and needs to be revived.

"In him was life, and the life was the light of all people." We need a renewal of that light, a renewal of the understanding it can give, a renewal of the caring it can stimulate, a renewal of the hope it sparks.

Finally, we could get from Christmas an enrichment of our personal relationship with the Christ of Christmas. We cannot exhaust the profound concepts that John puts forth in the introduction to this gospel. The more you read and study this passage, the more you are impressed by its depth and possibilities. John's main point is clear, however: The eternal, the inexplicable, the mysterious, has been revealed in a person, and we come to know God through a personal relationship with the divine.

"But to all who received him," John writes, "who believed in his name, he gave power to become children of God" (1:12). In a sense we are the children of God by creation, for God is the source and sustainer of all life, but we truly become the children of God only in relationship.

William Barclay illustrates the difference with this example. The name of a certain young man was mentioned to a noted teacher; the young man had claimed to be student of the teacher. The teacher replied, "He might have attended my lectures, but he was not one of my students." There's a world of difference between sitting in a teacher's classroom and being a student. Persons become students, followers, disciples, as they immerse themselves in the thought and method of their teacher. John claimed that persons become children of God through a life of trust and obedience toward Jesus Christ.

Why through Christ? According to John, in Christ the Word has been made flesh, and in him we discover the grace and truth of God. We can say that the Christ event occurred once for all in Jesus of Bethlehem, but it also occurs over and over in our experience. Jesus came; he also comes. Christmas reminds us of that fact, and summons us to a closer relationship with our Lord.

What will you get from Christmas? You can get renewal. You can get a fresh sense of wonder, a greater appreciation for the light, a closer relationship with Christ. But what you get depends on what you seek and on what you are ready to receive.

Day Five
"For God So Loved"

For this reason I bow my knees before the Father, from whom every family in heaven and on earth takes its name; I pray that according to the riches of his glory, he may grant that you may be strengthened in your inner being with power through his Spirit, and that Christ may dwell in your hearts through faith, as you are being rooted and grounded in love. I pray that you may have the power to comprehend, with all the saints, what is the breadth and length and height and depth, and to know the love of Christ that surpasses knowledge, so that you may be filled with all the fullness of God.
—(Eph 3:14-19)

We have no finer introduction to Christmas or to the Christ event than the simple, well-known words of John 3:16: "For God so loved the world that he gave his only son . . ." Preceding, underlying, and interpreting the coming of Christ is the love of God. In Jesus Christ we see what Paul called "the breadth and length and height and depth" of God's love.

What does God's love mean to people today? No one questions the affirmation that "God loves the world" or the concept that "God is love." These ideas we hear Sunday after Sunday, but how much do we understand about the love that we ascribe to God?

This question needs to be raised, because even though love is a common word in our vocabulary, it suffers extreme distortion. The popular notion of love as expressed in contemporary songs and novels, television shows and motion pictures, equates love with romance and sentimentality. Such an approach to love is basically self-centered and egoistic, for the word "love" is usually preceded by "I" and focuses on the wants and needs of the person speaking.

Even when human love is elevated to a higher plane, it is invariably selective and highly discriminating, limited to a favored few. We love persons, for example, who love us in return or who, we feel, deserve our love. We give love and then withhold it. We express it at times, and at other times we keep it inside. The inconsistent, limited, and distorted way we love or profess to love naturally leaves people wondering what we mean by love. It's as if the word has no meaning. Maybe we need a new word for love.

Our dilemma in regard to the word "love" is almost identical to that faced by the writers of the New Testament. They wanted to describe what they had discovered about God's love, and even though the language of their day had several terms for love, none was suitable to convey the love they had come to experience.

There was a word for romantic love, *eros,* but it was reserved for things that were lovely or attractive. There was a word for brotherly affection, *philea,* but it had to do with persons who were basically equal; it did not include outsiders. There was a word for affection within the family, *storge,* but it, too, was restricted to one's own group. So the New Testament writers resorted to a word for love that was seldom used, and they gave it a new definition. *Agape* love is based, not on the worthiness of the object of love, but on the decision of the subject to be loving. It is love that moves beyond sentimentality to deliberate action in behalf of its object.

This idea of love as spontaneous, unconditional, and active; this idea of love as that which always benefits and values its object; this idea of love as searching and irrepressible—this is what we mean when we talk about God's love. This idea of love stands in stark contrast to the notion of love so prevalent in our culture! Where else but in the Christ event do we find such love? Where else but in Christ can we receive it, learn it, and begin to practice it ourselves? "For God so loved . . ." "For God so loves . . ." It does have a present tense. Christmas reassures us of that. In celebrating the coming of Christ we are celebrating the reality of a searching, value-creating love that we need.

A beautiful example of this kind of love is portrayed in Lorraine Hansberry's play *A Raisin in the Sun.* The play is about a black family in Chicago's south side. The father of the household died, leaving a small legacy of $10,000 from an insurance policy. The mother wanted to use this money to move the children into a small house on the other side of town. She dreamed of a home of their own with shutters and window boxes filled with flowers.

Her son wanted the money to go into business. He had never had a chance, he said, never a "break" or a good job. A friend knew about a deal that would multiply the investment. Pathetically, he begged for the money. Gradually, the mother's resistance broke down, and she gave it to him. "You'll never regret this, Mother." He said, "We're going to be rich."

You can imagine what happened. Later, with head bowed and shoulders slumped, the son confessed that his "friend" had taken the money and skipped town. His sister, Beneatha, lost no time in tearing into him. She condemned him for being so stupid. She screamed at him for having lost the only escape route they had from the misery in which they had lived for years. When she had finished her tirade, the mother quietly said, "Beneatha, I thought I taught you to love your brother." "Love him?" she shouted back. "There is nothing left to love."

Then the mother said, "There's always something left to love. And if you ain't learned that, you ain't learned nothing. Have you cried for that boy today? I don't mean for the family 'cause we lost the money. I mean for him; what he's been through and what it done to him. Child, when do you think is the time to love some-body the most; when they done good and made things easy for everybody? Well, then, you ain't through learning—because that ain't the time at all. It's when he's at his lowest and can't believe in hisself 'cause the world done whipped him so. When you start measuring somebody, measure him right, child, measure him right. Make sure you done take into account what hills and valleys he come through before he got to wherever he is."

God loves us when we have done well, but the good news is that God loves us just as much when we have not done well, when we have messed up, when we have done terrible things, even when we have disgusted ourselves with our actions and attitudes. In spite of anything, God loves and values us. That kind of love goes far beyond popular concepts; yet, it is only a beginning to an understanding of the self-revelation God has made in Christ.

God's love not only penetrates any kind of circumstances; it also takes action. "For God so loved that he gave . . ." "For God so loves that he gives . . ." C. S. Lewis helped us immensely when he described the different kinds of love and called God's love "gift-love." Gift-love is quite simply the love that prompts us to give all that we are and all that we have, not through a need to be fulfilled, but through a desire to share. What has God given? God has given his Son, his "only begotten son," if you will. Lurking behind this expression is the mind-boggling truth that "God so loved the world that he gave himself." Gift-love is the giving of oneself.

We cannot live without this kind of love—not truly live! We can never be fully human or fully alive without it. C. S. Lewis also noted that we have a "need-love." We are poverty-stricken in this area, helpless. We need a love different from the loves we see in the world in order to become trusting, growing persons. We do not like to admit it (it runs counter to the image of strength and self-sufficiency we try hard to portray), but we all have a "need-love."

Bennett Cerf, the Random House publisher, once appeared on a panel discussing the topic, "What are you most afraid of?" Cerf provided very little to the vigorous exchange by the panelists. The consensus of the group was that the thing most to fear in the modern world is "annihilation by the bomb." Bennett Cerf was asked if he concurred. He said that he hesitated to answer the question truthfully because his concern might seem trivial in the light of the great issues introduced, but he added that since the point of the discussion was to share what one really thought, he might as well admit that "what he feared most was not being loved."

Gift-love and need-love—how do they relate? We cannot give to God what God gives to us. Indeed, that is not expected of us. God's selfless love yearns for a response, but we have only a selfish love. Remember, John does not say that God so loved the world that he gave his only son that whoever loves him . . . No, it says "whoever believes" or "trusts God's love"—that is the one who becomes able to love and learn gift-love. When it is genuine, it is received and multiplied many times over.

Day Six
From Nowhere to Everywhere

Long ago God spoke to our ancestors by the prophets, but in these last days he has spoken to us by a Son, whom he appointed heir of all things, through whom he also created the worlds. He is the reflection of God's glory and bears the exact imprint of God's very being, and he sustains all things by his powerful word. When he had made purification for sins, he sat down at the right hand of the Majesty on high, having become as much superior to angels as the name he has inherited is more excellent than theirs.
–(Heb 1:1-4)

One day I was scanning my bookshelves for something to read or to reread. I did not have long, so I wanted something that I could read in a short while. I pulled down a collection of works by American writers and settled on Ralph Waldo Emerson's essay called "The American Scholar." I had not read it since college. This essay was Emerson's Phi Beta Kappa address at Harvard, delivered in 1837. James Russell Lowell was present that day and made a striking comment about Emerson's lecture. He said that it "began nowhere and ended everywhere." He was referring, of course, to the simple thesis and broad application.

I have not been able to shake that expression: "It began nowhere and ended everywhere." How descriptive, it seems to me, of the coming of Christ! It "began nowhere"–in a dirty stable in an insignificant village in an obscure part of an empire long since gone–but it "ended everywhere." We need to appreciate the humble beginning of our Lord and our faith. We need also to visualize the immense meaning that Christ has for personal life, our world, and history.

We must have eyes to see, minds to understand, and hearts to appreciate that which comes into our experience. As we draw closer to the time when we celebrate the birth of our Lord Jesus Christ, we must sharpen our powers of perception so that we might not miss the significance of his coming.

From Bedlam to Bethlehem

Recognition, perception, and appreciation are extremely difficult for us. We have problems in these areas, because we have difficulty focusing our attention. What gets our attention gets us. Our attention is easily diverted from important matters by trivial concerns and distractions. We avoid them through self-centered pursuits. We fear what they might mean for us, but these things only indicate our need to get beyond them and direct our attention to the truly significant.

The writer of the letter to the Hebrews addressed readers with similar problems. They were distracted. The recipients of the letter were facing threats to their personal security; the church was beginning to undergo persecution. There was anxiety and worry, controversy within. Already, Christians were squabbling over beliefs. There was hostility and pettiness. Sin, pride, selfishness, and moral indifference were as real then as now. The attention of the congregation was not on Christ, so the writer of Hebrews began the letter by bringing Christ to the forefront.

Concentrate first, the writer was saying, on what is of supreme importance, and everything else will find its place. The letter began: "Long ago God spoke to our ancestors by the prophets, but in these last days he has spoken to us by a Son." In the child of Bethlehem God has spoken finally and fully. Let nothing cloud that fact or crowd it out! If the author of Hebrews were writing the modern church and aware of our situation, would the letter to us not begin in the same way? Do not let the season or the celebration get in the way of the truth that is celebrated. Brush away the trivial; look beyond your worries; focus your attention on the heart of it all!

Preparation is important. God did not send God's own Son without adequate preparation. Through the centuries God prepared the way. God spoke through Moses and through Moses gave the law, a major step in the interaction between God and God's people. The law became a light and a guide for Israel, but the law was insufficient.

God spoke through the prophets. One by one they came with rays of light and glimpses of truth. The prophetic tradition was so dynamic that even today it rattles our complacency with calls to

24

justice, honesty, and social responsibility. Who can fail to be moved by Amos' appeal for social justice, Isaiah's concept of God's holiness, or Hosea's experience of forgiving love? The law and the prophets were much like decorations, however. They were partial, fragmentary. God has spoken ultimately in Jesus Christ our Lord. With intense spiritual and literary power, the writer of Hebrews wanted to say: Don't let that truth be dimmed, either in your own thinking or in the world! Recognize it for what it is!

Jesus Christ, the writer proclaims, is God's "final" word. By "final" the writer did not mean that Christ is last in a series of statements or that God no longer speaks. By "final" the writer meant that Christ is the decisive, fulfilling, unsurpassed disclosure of what God is like and who God is. John wrote:

> The law indeed was given through Moses; grace and truth came through Jesus Christ. No one has ever seen God. It is God the only Son, who is close to the Father's heart, who has made him known (1:17-18).

Most of our religious discussions, sermons, and meditations center on what Jesus said or perhaps what he did—which is appropriate. His teachings and his example provide our guide to faith and ethics, but we must remember who he was, who he is: God in human flesh, God with us, God's final gift. Who Christ is contains the key to Christian faith and celebration. You can miss that if you're not careful.

Also, this New Testament writer claimed, "He is the reflection of God's glory." "God's glory" is an expression that leads us to think in terms of some awesome display of power and grandeur. Indeed, an angelic chorus, at the birth of Jesus, sang, "Glory to God in the highest" (Luke 2:14); but after the angels went away, there was no more singing. Did the glory disappear? Not at all!

The glory Jesus demonstrated was not a spectacular heavenly display, but a glory found when men and women, boys and girls are set free from the power of sin, a glory found in sacrifice and deeds of love and mercy, a glory found in sincere prayer, a glory found in the home where Christ is the head, a glory found in the genuine fellowship of the Christian community. A quiet glory, but a glory—which you will miss if you are looking for the spectacular.

The Son, we read here, is the "exact imprint of God's very being." The imagery is that of a king's seal that leaves an exact impression in soft, warm wax. When the wax hardens, there remains the precise reproduction of the seal or stamp. The message is clear. If you want to know what God is like, you do not have to speculate. You simply look at Christ, not at theological pronouncements, but at the action of Christ in the world. We see in Jesus Christ that God not only speaks; God does. Talking and backing talk with action are two different things.

Samuel Woolman, whose son, John, became widely known for his writings on the discipline of the inner life, was an eighteenth-century New Jersey Quaker. In his village one day, a neighbor with whom Samuel had been talking was starting home. At the edge of town, the horse, on which the neighbor and his little farm depended, slumped to the ground and died. People gathered. One man, known as actively religious, spoke words aimed at comfort, "It's just too bad. How sorry I am." Samuel Woolman said nothing, but without losing eye contact with the man who spoke, he slowly drew his purse from his pocket. "I'm five dollars sorry," he said. "How sorry are you?" Christ, "the imprint of God's very being" shows how much God cares.

As if these statements about the Christ are not startling enough, the writer of Hebrews said that he "sustains all things by his powerful word." This person obviously had a deep appreciation for the concept of providence. The writer did not think of God as creating the world and then leaving it to itself, but saw a divine purpose in history. The author saw the emergence of the kingdom Christ came to inaugurate.

We need this attitude toward history and events. Indeed, I hope that we can all see that what seemed to begin nowhere does end everywhere, that Christ has meaning for every life and every situation. What an impact his coming would make if we related our questions to him, if we could share our problems with him, if we could commit our loved ones to his keeping!

The Christ event began nowhere and ended everywhere. Our faith suffers if we forget either of those truths, if we try to make it so sophisticated or "spiritual" that we take away the "God in humanity" of it all or if we timidly refuse to acknowledge the cosmic dimensions of the lordship of Christ, that "the kingdoms of this world are become the kingdoms of our God and of his Christ." Let's not miss the central point of Christmas. Let's hear God's "final" word; let's rejoice in God's universal reign.

Day Seven
Have a Childlike Christmas!

People were bringing little children to him in order that he might touch them; and the disciples spoke sternly to them. But when Jesus saw this, he was indignant and said to them, "Let the children come to me; do not stop them; for it is to such as these that the kingdom of God belongs. Truly I tell you, whoever does not receive the kingdom of God as a little child will never enter it." And he took them up in his arms, laid his hands on them, and blessed them.

—(Mark 10:13-16)

Almost every day now you hear the adage, "Christmas is for children." I suppose this statement means that adults are so concerned with busyness and expenses that they merely hope to muddle through the season, while children, the recipients of so many efforts, are better able to enjoy all that is going on. Perhaps it implies that adults are so preoccupied with work and on-going problems that they cannot afford to stop to experience the beauty and consider the meaning of what we celebrate. Whatever we mean, there is something unfortunate about this comment.

You recall that during his ministry children were often brought to Jesus. Parents who were touched by the presence of our Lord and moved by his words wanted their little ones to have contact with him and to receive his blessing. On one occasion, as parents and children were coming to Jesus, the disciples tried to turn them away. The disciples were not actually being cruel; they wanted to protect Jesus from distractions. They knew that he had much on his mind, important work to do, and they did not want him bothered.

This instance was one of the few times when Jesus became angry. He rebuked his followers: "Let the little children come to me; do not stop them." As he spoke to, and perhaps played with, the children, he turned to the grown-ups standing by and said,

"Truly I tell you, whoever does not receive the kingdom of God as a little child will never enter it."

I think Jesus' rebuke might extend beyond his disciples to include all persons who are so caught up in work and worry that they cannot enjoy his presence and relate to him in a trusting way. Is Christmas for children? If it is, then let us be children. Let the child within us come to the surface so that we might worship the Christ with simplicity and purity of heart. Maybe we can learn some things from our children, or perhaps I should say, maybe we can recapture some things.

From children we can learn a sense of wonder and awe. The adult mind is drawn to explanations. It should be, for we should try to understand what happens in our lives and in our world and why. Every year about this time without fail, we attempt again to explain the Incarnation. The question that Anselm raised, *Cur Deus Homo?* or "Why the God-Man?" summons forth our best theological efforts. When we have said what we can, however, we have to confess that something about Christmas transcends the mind and reaches into the heart and that we need a childlike spirit to understand it.

I think Walt Whitman described this attitude of wonder and awe quite well:

> When I heard the learn'd astronomer,
> When the proofs, the figures, were ranged in columns before me,
> When I was shown the charts and diagrams,
> to add, divide, and measure them,
> When I heard the astronomer where he lectured with
> much applause in the lecture-room,
> How soon unaccountable I became tired and sick,
> Till rising and gliding out I wander'd off by myself,
> In the mystical moist night-air, and from time to time,
> Looked up in perfect silence at the stars.[3]

Chevis Horne, a former pastor in Virginia, said that at the close of the kindergarten year at his church, the children were taken to the city park for a picnic. One little boy, keenly aware of the vast sky above him and the tall trees about him, exclaimed, "God wonders me!" The exclamation of this child, Horne said,

29

may not be perfect English, but it is a perfect expression of the wonder and mystery that surround Christmas.

God has "wondered" us in sending his Son. God has shown the depth and extent of divine love that brings reconciliation. We cannot fully explain this wonder nor fully appreciate it apart from a childlike sense of awe. We need to give way to that spirit.

Children also have a special way of getting to the heart of things. They have not yet learned to conceal their true feelings or to hide their fears. Their questions are pointed and direct, as any mother can attest. While adults fret with the trappings of Christmas, children want to know what it all means. Why so much trouble? What are we really doing?

Leonard Griffith once told a delightful story about a group of English school children constructing a manger scene in the corner of their classroom. They built the barn and covered the floor with hay. The figures of Mary, Joseph, the shepherds, the Wise Men, and the animals were all facing the little straw bed. A tiny doll represented the baby Jesus. The children were excited, but one little fellow seemed troubled. He returned again and again to the corner of the room to study the manger scene. Finally, the teacher asked if something was wrong. Revealing wisdom typical of a child's ability to confound the wise, he said, "What I'd like to know is–where does God fit in?"

The little boy's question is a good one for a time so laden with customs and commercialization. Christmas for many people is not really a religious observance at all, but rather an old Norse festival slightly modified by a nominally Christian society. "Where does God fit in?" Where does God fit in our observance? We must answer individually, but before the adult rationalizations begin and we resort to our excuses about not having time and having too much on our minds, let's allow the child within us to ask and answer this direct question.

Perhaps Jesus delighted in children and encouraged the child-like attitude because children are dependent and trusting. They look to their parents for all of their needs. Children are willing to receive. They do not feel that they have to do everything for themselves.

This childlike mind and spirit, Jesus said, is necessary to receive the kingdom of God. This is a challenging and disturbing statement. The Pharisees, for example, could not receive the Kingdom. Though they professed to be God-fearers, they were characterized by self-conscious goodness and spiritual arrogance. With their good deeds as evidence of their righteousness, they had literally outgrown their need for God. How could they understand Jesus' talk about a loving heavenly Father who feeds the birds and clothes the lilies of the field in splendor?

We should not be surprised that the religious community at the time of Jesus' birth failed to recognize his coming. To be sure, the religious leaders knew the prophecies: "Look, the young woman is with child and shall bear a son, and shall name him Immanuel" (Isa 7:14); "For a child has been born for us, a son given to us" (Isa 9:6); "But you, O Bethlehem of Ephrathah, . . . shall come forth for me one who is to rule in Israel" (Mic 5:2). The vision had faded, however. The childlike spirit of anticipation had been lost. Unable to wait for God's time and God's way, the Jewish religious leaders decided to do things their own way. There was no room in their scheme of things for a baby.

It has been said that you and I live in a world today that has "come of age," a secular world, a grown-up world. It is also a cynical world, a world lacking in sympathy and humanitarian concern. One needs only listen to the current news to realize this truth.

Do we not need a childlike sense of trust in the purposes of God to discover again this Christmas that God still has plans for us? Over against the brutality and oppression we hear about in many countries, the message of "peace on earth, good will among men" resounds. Over against the reality of hungry multitudes and economic perplexities, we still hear the message of hope. Are we childlike to maintain such hope and to pray to such ends? Are we childlike to confess our own ineptness to handle the problems we have created and to look to a heavenly Father for deliverance? If so, maybe we need childlikeness.

Jesus also praised in the childlike attitude the capacity to respond with spontaneity and gratitude. Make a gift or show a kindness to children and they accept what you do wholehearted-ly. They are not skeptical about your intentions; they do not ask about "strings" that might be attached.

Jesus always welcomed the ready response, such as Peter's confession of faith and the woman's breaking the vial of precious ointment. Of course, he wanted men and women to consider his call very carefully, to think things through. Yet, at a point cautious consideration becomes simple indecision, a point at which analy-sis of possibilities becomes paralysis of action. The church can become guilty of this inaction.

A leap of faith is involved in following Christ, and while I would advise anyone to look before leaping, there is still the leap, the act of trust. Are we childlike simply to hear the call of Christ and to follow? Jesus said, "Whoever does not receive the kingdom of God like a child shall not enter it."

"Christmas is for children." Perhaps it takes childlike qualities to understand it, appreciate it, and respond to it. Let us then be children. Have a childlike Christmas!

Notes

[1]John Mason, 1851. "O Come, O Come, Emmanuel." Tune VENI EMMANUEL, adapted from Plainsong by Thomas Helmore, 1854.

[2]Hugh C. Warner, *Daily Readings from William Temple* (Nashville: Abingdon Press, 1950) 271–72.

[3]Walt Whitman, *Leaves of Grass*, "When I Heard the Learn'd Astronomer" (New York: Penguin Books USA Inc., 1980) 226.

The Second
Week of Advent

What's in a Name?

Day One
The Miracle of Becoming

*And the Word became flesh and lived among us, and we have seen his glory,
the glory as of a father's only son, full of grace and truth.*

—(John 1:14)

One of my seminary professors had a deep concern, not only for the theological understanding of his students, but also for their ability to express their views. Each time he graded and returned our papers, he would spend a class period reviewing them. Frequently he would say, "Be direct and precise in your writing. Get to the point. Especially be careful in your use of verbs."

I think of that professor's advice when I read John's four-word description of the Incarnation, "The Word became flesh." Consider John's brevity and choice of verbs. A verb expresses an act, an occurrence, or a mode of being. To depict the supreme event of history, John chose the simplest of verbs. Yet, we should not hurry over it, for the most profound is often best described in the simplest of terms. I suggest that the familiar verb "become" in its past, present, and future tenses is the best of words to tell the beautiful story of what God has done and continues to do in Jesus Christ. I would even say that it describes a miracle, for becoming is a miracle.

According to *Webster's New Collegiate Dictionary,* the primary meaning of become is "to come into existence." John said flatly that the Word, the *Logos,* has come into existence as we know it as flesh. He employed a favorite philosophical term. Logos in Greek meant "reason." It represented the external reason or wisdom, uncaused and unexplainable, that lay behind the created order. To Greek thinkers it was an impersonal principle. Hebrew scholars spoke of the Logos as the creating, guiding, and directing power of God in history, the very mind and wisdom of God.

John's statement bluntly proclaims that in the coming of Jesus Christ God's mind, purpose, and love became human. Can you imagine what a radical affirmation that was (and still is!)? Almost every thinker of John's day was willing to accept the idea of the Logos, but it was inconceivable that God would become human.

To many people God was in the heavens unconcerned with the world and undisturbed by its dark problems. Some philosophers thought it blasphemy to say that God would become involved in the affairs of the world. Others said that the life of God has not descended to us, nor has it come as far as the necessities of the body. After the time of Christ, toward the end of the first century, when John was writing his gospel, many persons even in the Christian church were wondering whether the divine had actually become human. Perhaps, they said, Jesus only seemed to be a man.

The miraculous has always given us trouble. We want to be able to understand and explain things. Mystery frightens us. We prefer to avoid that which has no rational solution. We want no one to think we are naive. Unfortunately, even when Christians talk about the miraculous, they get sidetracked by incidentals. It's not hard, for example, to initiate a lively discussion about the "virgin birth." Frankly, I've never had much interest in that. For me John put his finger on something far more important. Whether Jesus was born of a virgin or not (by the way, if you're wondering, I believe that he was) is not nearly as significant as the truth that in him God became human.

Luke said that Jesus became a man. The child Jesus does not disturb us; we are attracted to the innocence and helplessness of an infant. The baby Jesus does not threaten the power structures of our world, but the child became a man who said: "Follow me" (Mark 1:17); "Seek first the kingdom of God" (Matt 6:33); "Go . . . do not sin again" (John 8:11); "You cannot serve God and wealth" (Matt 6:24). The child became the man who questioned the way we do business, the way we relate to God, and the way we relate to each other.

Paul said that this man who knew no sin "was made to be sin . . . so that in him we might become the righteousness of God" (2 Cor 5:21). Taking our sin, guilt, and burden upon himself, he became our Savior. Every part of this being and work of Jesus

35

Christ can be described as nothing less than miraculous. In Jesus the Word became flesh; something wholly beyond our range of understanding came into existence.

Now consider the second dictionary meaning of this verb "become" and move to the present tense. Not only does it mean "to come into existence"; it means "to undergo change or development." Because the Word became flesh, because Jesus became Savior, we are able to become or to undergo change. How does John put it? "But to all who received him (Christ), who believed in his name, he gave power to become children of God" (1:12). That's a miracle, too—an extraordinary occurrence, well beyond the boundaries of rational explanation, that takes place within us when we enter a faith relationship with Jesus Christ.

What happens within us is not a mild transformation of personality but an essential change of nature. We become a new creation, with new aims and standards, new likes and dislikes, new possibilities and powers. We undergo this change, not by osmosis or through natural development, but through belief in or through a faith relationship with Christ.

Every year at this time we talk about recovering the "true meaning of Christmas," about getting past the commercialism and the busyness and getting down to what Christmas is all about. Maybe we can do that by thinking not only about what Jesus Christ became but also about what we are becoming in him.

Recently I read the testimony of a college professor who was near retirement when he began to ask who Jesus Christ really is. For forty years he had taught on campus. He had read many books about the Christian faith. He had never opposed it; he had simply been indifferent and skeptical of anything that sounded miraculous. He said: "I suppose I chose to ignore Christ. He seemed to me to be just another prophet. This attitude led me into a personal wilderness. I tried to satisfy my inner needs by reading and by studying literature and science."

One day a student asked directly, "Are you a Christian?" The professor said that he had not considered the question since childhood. The student invited him to a campus service where the speaker talked about Christ not as prophet and teacher but as savior. "Before he was half through," the professor said, "I was convinced. A lifetime's assumption that Jesus was just another gifted teacher was destroyed. The turnabout in my convictions was easy."

Well, the turnabout is not always easy. To be correct I would have to say that it rarely is. We have to be ready for a miracle to take place within us; and miracles, we think, are few and far between today. We do not want to be viewed as superstitious or gullible. Yet, the craving for the miraculous continues. Dostoyevsky once said, "Man cannot bear to be without the miraculous." He added that if a person does not discover miracles from God, "he will create miracles of his own for himself."

We have our "miracles"–advanced technology to give us a sense of power, drugs to give us a sense of well-being, things to give us a sense of security, self-styled memorials to give us a sense of permanence. Do these things not stem from a craving for the miraculous? The genuinely miraculous is actually much more simple; the greatest miracle we can experience is the miracle of becoming.

What have we become in the light of what Christ became? Take that thought to the future tense, for the Christ event is a continuing miracle. What shall we become? That question stopped Ebenezer Scrooge in his tracks and made him seek transformation. Because life in Christ has goals, because we are to move toward maturity, we have to speak of what we "shall become." The awesome, sobering truth is that unless we experience changes and redirections along our pilgrimage, we will become more of what we are now. Thoughts, unchanged, will become more rigidly fixed. Sins, unrepented of, will become more tyrannical. Fears, unmet, will become more enslaving. If we are unhappy with ourselves now, we cannot expect age or experience alone to improve things.

We need change, transformation, reorientation; in short, we need to become–to become like the one who became one of us to give us a model, an example, a pattern to follow. He was the Son of God. He was a miracle. He could be loving, free, courageous, and committed! We are different! Are we? Does John not say that all who believe on him become children of God? Did Jesus himself not say that he is a brother to anyone who does the will of God? Does the New Testament not say that he is the first in a family of faith? A miracle is involved here, something outside the realm of our understanding. It is the miracle of becoming—the miracle of what Jesus became, what we are becoming, and what we shall become.

Day Two
Finding Christ in Christmas

"Where is the child who has been born king of the Jews? For we have observed his star at its rising, and have come to pay him homage." When Herod the king heard this, he was troubled, and all Jerusalem with him.
—(Matt 2:2-3)

When I was growing up, a large manufacturing concern in my hometown put up a display in front of its plant each Christmas. Usually, it was a nativity scene, with figures of the holy parents standing by a manger, awestruck shepherds, and adoring wise men. Over the scene was a banner that read, "Merry Christmas." One year the theme changed. Spotlighted on the lawn was a living room containing a brightly decorated tree and a hearth with stockings. This time the central figure was Santa Claus, rummaging through a big bag of presents. The banner read, "Merry X-mas and Happy New Year." I still recall the critical comment of people in my community: "They've taken Christ out of Christmas." For the first time I became aware of that statement. I've heard it many times since then.

We cannot actually take Christ out of Christmas, but we can push him aside and make concentration on him extremely difficult. Through the years, I suppose, we have made Christmas an increasingly elaborate ritual and, in doing so, we have pushed Christ farther and farther from the center. Thus, sometimes we talk about "putting Christ back into Christmas." We realize our need to revitalize or perhaps redirect our celebration of the Christ event.

I hear some novel suggestions for "putting Christ back into Christmas." A friend wrote in his church newsletter that maybe we should change the time of our observance of the birth of Christ. He recommended that we have Christmas in August. "Nothing happens in August," he wrote. "It's too hot to do anything in August." He went on to say:

> No one would write sentimental secular songs about Christmas in August to distract us from worship. I doubt if "I'm Dreaming of a Heat Wave" could ever gain the following of "I'm Dreaming of a White Christmas." Surely "Corn Cob the Scarecrow" would never catch the imagination like "Frosty the Snowman." In August we would not have to compete with all the romantic images conjured up by phrases like "Chestnuts Roasting on an Open Fire." There is nothing romantic about "hamburgers burning on a charcoal grill."

This suggestion and most of our other ideas for changing the way we observe Christmas are hardly likely to be taken seriously. It remains for us to make a special effort to remember what is important about this season and do what we can to "put Christ into Christmas" or to find Christ amid all the distractions and diversions. It is worth the effort.

Finding Christ has been a part of Christmas since the beginning. We think of the search for him each time we read Matthew's lovely story of the magi who appeared in Jerusalem during the reign of Herod the Great asking, "Where is he who has been born king of the Jews?" Their search began a quest that continues to the present day. We are still trying to find the Christ.

From the first, Christ was pushed to the periphery of things. He was a cause of trouble. His coming indicated change. Instead of being an occasion for rejoicing, his presence was a disturbance. Herod was disturbed; the mention of another king was a threat. The priests and scribes were disturbed; the actual coming of the messiah would threaten their tight, cozy control on religion. While feigning interest in the Christ, their minds were so preoccupied with their own concerns that they, for all practical purposes, "took Christ out of Christmas." The whole process has a contemporary ring. Give lip service, but look after "number one."

Something here perplexes me every time I read this account: the fact that the priestly scholars, who knew the prophecies concerning the messiah and could locate the place where he was to be born, did not even have the curiosity to travel the few miles from Jerusalem to Bethlehem with distinguished visitors from another land to see whether there was substance in what they said. If indifference can take Christ out of Christmas, this is a classic case!

The magi searched, but not without help. They followed the star that had initiated their journey, and the star "went before them, till it came to rest over the place where the child was." I frankly don't know how to explain this celestial sign or the kind of guidance that pointed the magi to the place in Bethlehem where Mary and Joseph were keeping their child. Some people say that we could easily find Christ if we had something so dramatic to capture our attention.

I am not certain, however, that the star alone enabled the magi to find the Christ. I am impressed by their single-minded concentration. They were not deterred by the distance from their home to Bethlehem, nor discouraged by the rigors of desert travel, nor deviated by the treachery of Herod and his court. They had firmly in their hearts and minds a desire to find the newborn king. They would not be distracted. Nothing could, if I may use a modern expression, "take Christ out of Christmas" for them.

What enabled the magi to find Christ is still required: single-minded concentration and a willingness to follow the leads we have. We see no visible star, but there are lights around and within us every bit as bright as the star of the wise men. Look first for Christ in your own situation and experience, as ordinary as things might seem to you. You do not have to "go" anywhere to find Christ. After all, that's what Christmas is all about–the fact that the "Word became flesh," that God came in Jesus Christ "born of flesh," that God is with us.

I realize that finding Christ in our mundane, everyday existence is difficult. We face many distractions: selfish concerns, fears, feelings of guilt, ambition, and so on. If we do not find Christ in these areas of our lives, we will not find him. Somewhere in every life is a star that shines to indicate the presence of Christ. If we follow its light with genuine concentration, we will find the Christ.

Look for Christ in others. Listen for him in their longings. Feel his pain in their needs. "Truly I tell you," he once declared, "just as you did it to one of the least of these who are members of my family, you did it to me" (Matt 25:40). Look for Christ among his people. "For where two or three are gathered in my name," he said, "I am among them" (Matt 18:20). Look for him in deeds of kindness and generosity, for his spirit prompts sincere giving. Look for him in the impulse to share or to serve, in the tug of the heart that seems so strong, at this time of year.

A constellation of stars points the way to the Christ. We cannot take Christ out of Christmas. He is there, but not everyone will find him. We must move beyond the distractions, beyond personal preoccupations. We must fix our attention and eyes on him.

During the days of the Persian ruler Cyrus the Great, a political resister named Cagular lived on the southern border of the vast empire. This chieftain consistently defeated the small detachments of Cyrus' army that were sent to subdue him. Finally, the emperor sent his whole army, and the chieftain Cagular was captured. He and his family were brought to the capital for trial and execution. On the appointed day, they stood in the judgment hall before Cyrus.

Cyrus was impressed by this handsome and fearless man, his noble wife, and his two beautiful children. Finally, Cyrus said, "What would you do, Cagular, if I should spare your life?" "Your majesty," came the reply, "if you spared my life I would return to my home and remain your obedient servant as long as I live." Cyrus asked, "What would you do if I should spare the lives of your children?" "Your majesty, if you spared the lives of my children I would gather my scattered horde, place your banner over them, and lead them to victory on many fields of battle."
Cyrus asked, "And what would you do if I spared the life of your wife?" "Your majesty, if you spared the life of my wife, I would die for you."

So moved was the emperor that he freed them all and returned Cagular to his province to act as governor. On the way home, Cagular asked his wife, "Did you notice the marble at the entrance of the palace, the different colors, and the figures so perfectly formed?" "No" she said, "I did not notice the marble." "Did you notice the tapestry on the wall of the corridor outside the great hall? It was magnificent!" "No," she said "I did not notice the tapestry." "Surely you noticed the emperor's throne. It seemed to have been carved from one lump of gold." "No," she said, "I did not notice the throne." Cagular asked, "Did you see nothing?" She answered, "On the way in I was too full of fear to see, and on the way out I beheld only the face of the man who said he would die for me."

I don't know what you see at Christmas, but there is much to see and discover. In it all is the one who came to be with us and to give his life for us. If we see everything else and fail to find him in Christmas, God help us.

Day Three
A Name for the Child:
"Wonderful Counselor"

For a child has been born for us, a son given to us; authority rests upon his shoulders; and he is named "Wonderful Counselor, Mighty God, Everlasting Father, Prince of Peace."

—(Isa 9:6)

Advent prepares us to celebrate the birth of a child. Nothing else in human experience can compare with the birth of a baby. Even in our jaded scientific age, we call birth a miraculous event. It remains something that arouses deep joy and fervent hope. When a child is born, we almost always ask the same questions and almost always in the same sequence: Are the mother and child all right? Is it a boy or a girl? What is its name? During Advent we think about the third question in regard to the baby born in Bethlehem. What is the name of the child whose coming we so lavishly celebrate?

In biblical times, names were highly significant. A name was chosen to predict a person's character or to describe his or her personality. Sometimes a name was changed to denote a change in a person's life or calling. For example, Abram, after his calling to a covenant relationship with God, was renamed Abraham, which meant "father of a multitude." At birth, the second son of Isaac was named Jacob, or "supplanter," or "trickster." In maturity he became known as Israel, or "he who strives with God." Hannah named her son Samuel, which meant "asked for." Elijah the prophet had a name that meant "Jehovah is my God."

We do well, therefore, to give attention to the name of the child born to Mary and Joseph. We know him, of course, as Jesus, Savior, Christ, "Anointed One," but there is much more to his name. Perhaps the Bible contains many names for our Lord because no one name captures the essence of his person and work.

A beautiful passage in the prophecy of Isaiah helps us in the naming process. Isaiah lived in a period of national and spiritual disintegration. He saw the futility of temple worship and recognized that injustice and paganism were sapping the strength of Judah. He became certain of an impending national collapse. Yet Isaiah was equally convinced that God was at work. Even as he spoke of a people walking in darkness, he could also envision the appearance of a "great light." The victory, he said, would come in the birth of a child—"For a child has been born for us, a son is given"—and he gave the child names.

Isaiah did not name children arbitrarily. His prophetic messages were enshrined in the names of his own sons. They virtually had sermon titles for names. His first-born was called Shear-jashub, which meant "a remnant shall return." A second son was named Maher-shalal-hash-baz, or "the spoil speeds, the destruction hastens." Names were important to Isaiah. We need to note his suggestions for a name for the Christ child.

His name will be called, "Wonderful Counselor, Mighty God, Everlasting Father, Prince of Peace." Old Testament scholars call these "throne names," titles given to a king or exalted ruler. Yet, as we study and reflect on these names, we find that they have a deep personal meaning for everyone who comes to see the child. They touch our faith and aid our understanding.

The first name on Isaiah's list is Wonderful Counselor. The literal meaning is "a wonder of a counselor." Isaiah probably had in mind a counselor, planner, or administrator in the tradition of Solomon, a leader with wisdom and vision. If we make this name personal and bring it into the present, it becomes a name of rare beauty and meaning.

Basically, counseling is the art of sharing, guiding, and supporting. At its best it relies on an intensely personal relationship, an I-Thou relationship. It involves honesty and trust, which are required for any meaningful sharing of oneself. Everyone needs a counselor, another human being with whom we can share feelings and fears, with whom we can speak openly and honestly. An old Celtic proverb says it well: "Anyone without a soul-friend is a body without a head." I find it remarkable that we should discover, in this technological age of all times, the profound need we all have for a counselor, a friend of the soul.

In this context Isaiah's name for the child of Bethlehem takes on immense significance. If we enter into relationship with him, if we seek to grow under his care, he becomes for us a Wonderful Counselor. He relates to us with understanding, compassion, and encouragement. The child anticipated by Isaiah was born a real human being. He grew up the way real human beings grow. He felt pain, sorrow, fatigue, discouragement, loneliness, and eventually rejection. The writer of Hebrews could say, "For we do not have a high priest who is unable to sympathize with our weaknesses, but we have one who in every respect has been tempted as we are" (4:15). This counselor understands our experiences, because his own have run the gamut of human problems. He does not hear us with detachment; he even seeks to make entrance into our lives. The other day I ran across an interesting question posed by a motivational writer. He asked why Joseph Kennedy's sons excelled while Franklin Roosevelt's did not? Part of the answer to that riddle, he speculated, can be found in Franklin Roosevelt Jr.'s remark that an appointment was always required if he wanted to see his father. One day, when the boy had a pressing problem, FDR listened to his son but never stopped working at his desk. When the boy stopped talking, FDR said absently, "Glad you could drop by," and the interview was over. On the other hand, for all his shortcomings, Joseph Kennedy displayed constant interest in and loyalty to his children. He said, "My family is my business, and my business is my family." Once John Kennedy told a reporter, "You know, when I was just trying out for the freshman swim team, my dad was there. He was always there. He did the same for all the kids."

Always there! Always interested! "I am with you always" (Matt 28:20); "I will never leave you or forsake you" (Heb 13:5). Is Christ that kind of soul-friend to you, one on whom you can always rely, one who is always there not judging, not condemning, but ready to help? I perceive Jesus Christ in that way. To call him Wonderful Counselor seems a natural thing. He understands.

Christ also directs. He confronts us with the truth about ourselves. A counselor who merely hears our problems and gives us a pat on the ego does not deserve the title. Persons seek a counselor because they see the need to change their behavior or deal with some problem. Not only do we need a soul-friend, but we need to be responsible and accountable to that friend. People who attach themselves to a particular set of friends, a counselor, a therapy group, or a study or prayer group do so because they want to change and grow. They want honestly to share their burdens; they want an honest response.

This honest direction accounts for the success of Alcoholics Anonymous. Persons with alcohol dependency come to AA seeking help. They confess who they are. They are not condemned; they are accepted. They find community and understanding, but they also become accountable. The combination of acceptance and accountability brings healing.

This element of acceptance and accountability in our relationship with Christ needs emphasis. Our Lord said, "The truth will make you free." That which liberates sometimes hurts, but our Counselor is truthful with us. He did not condemn the woman taken in adultery, but he said, "Go . . . do not sin again" (John 8:11). He took a quick liking to the rich young ruler, but he said, "You lack one thing; go, sell what you own, and give the money to the poor" (Mark 10:21). He felt instant pity for the paralytic who had lived for years by the pool of Bethzatha, but he told the man he would have to want to get well (John 5:6).

This counselor knows the truth about us and confronts us with this truth. Indeed, he will not let us live with falsehood. This counselor also helps us with our problems. Much to our dismay, he does not solve them for us. Rather, he gives us the strength to face them ourselves. He will not deliver us from trouble; rather, he makes us sufficient for the troubles we face. He called men and women to be followers or disciples. Those who responded to his call he referred to as friends. To each one of them he gave himself completely. Yet, each also had his/her own cross to bear. This counselor calls us to be fully human. He hears us, confronts us, encourages us, and remains within us.

Day Four
A Name for the Child:
"Mighty God"

I
f you have never read Barbara Robinson's book called *The Best Christmas Pageant Ever*, I recommend it to you. In that story the rowdy Herdman kids, known by their schoolmates as the "horrible Herdmans," took over the Sunday School Christmas pageant. The six of them forced their way into the main roles. Ralph took the part of Joseph, Imogene played Mary, Gladys was an angel, and three younger brothers were wise men. During the first rehearsal a question arose about the naming of the Christ child. On cue, one character spoke up, quoting Isaiah, "His name shall be called Wonderful Counselor, Mighty God, Everlasting Father, Prince of Peace." Imogene Herdman had never heard that. Her big-eyed response was, "My goodness, what a name! He'd never get out of the first grade if he had to write all that."

Many names are given in the Bible for the child of Bethlehem. They are not given to confuse, but to enlighten, to help us understand and know him. Isaiah's second suggestion of a name for this child is "Mighty God." Somehow, of the four given in this text, this one seems to be least fitting. "Mighty God" also means "mighty hero" or "warrior." It refers to power, supremacy, and authority. It's hard to apply such a name to a helpless baby born in a stable to poor parents. Even today, with our advantage of historical perspective, we find it difficult to think of the Christ child as "Mighty God," for his life did not coincide with the kind of authoritarian, coercive strength that the term implies.

Yet, even if we wonder about the appropriateness of this name, there is no question about its appeal. We like the concept of a Mighty God. The aim of religion is to make and to maintain contact with a God who is all-knowing, all-seeing, and all-powerful; a God who can and will deliver people out of all their troubles; a God who makes things right and establishes justice with a mighty hand. We are drawn to the idea of a hero or warrior who cannot be defeated. Yes, this is a good name, though it does seem a little improbable.

The prophet Isaiah, no doubt, rejoiced to share his vision concerning the coming of one who would reveal God's might. He spoke of living in a land of deep darkness, bearing the rod of the oppressor, hearing the tramp of soldiers' boots. He was thinking, of course, of the fearsome threat of Assyrian armies, poised to overrun his people. His words reach far beyond the situation of Jerusalem in the eighth century B.C., however. Isaiah speaks for everyone who has ever felt surrounded by darkness.

Isaiah needed a Mighty God, and so do we. We live in a world dark with oppression, injustice, ignorance, and deprivation. We face a world of overwhelming need. We are no less aware of darkness in our personal lives. We need the idea of a Mighty God to deal with our own problems and difficulties. I am convinced that, despite all of the things that distract us during this season, we come back to Advent and Christmas to experience a renewal of hope that our Mighty God will bring liberation and peace and establish a kingdom of justice and righteousness. Yes, Mighty God is a good name for the child.

What does this name, Mighty God, mean? Obviously, it refers to a God of might, of power. But how is the power shown? Power is a subject about which much is said and written today. Current news stories deal with nuclear power, military power, and economic power. We speak of power over persons, power over situations, and power over oneself. Basically, however, there are but two kinds of power: political and spiritual. To know the child who is called Mighty God, we have to make a distinction.

According to the legends that developed in connection with the birth of Buddha, soothsayers informed Buddha's father that his child would grow up to become the most powerful king in the land or else a poor man who would be the greatest spiritual leader his people had ever known—either/or, but not both.

The legend about Buddha contains profound wisdom. One opts for political might, which is the capacity to coerce others to do his will, or he chooses spiritual power, which resides in love and giving. I know of no distinction that is more helpful in pointing us to the mightiness of God in Christ. The child is the Mighty God. In him God has revealed God's self and power. This is not a political power, nor a coercive or deterministic power, nor one that is arbitrary or vindictive power. This child is the Mighty God in love, humility, giving, and vulnerability. We find difficulty in understanding and trusting this kind of power because it transcends anything we experience.

Notice how God's might is expressed in this child. We cannot overlook the humility of his arrival. He did not come as a prince in line for a kingdom and an army. He came as a helpless, defenseless baby, vulnerable to hurt. The very humility of Jesus' birth tips us off that something majestic is associated with it. Had the child expressed material power, we would worship the power we could see, but since there are no outward trappings of might, we learn to look beyond the visible and the material. The child tells us not to trust in this world but to trust in God.

Alexander Solzhenitzen said that when he was in prison, at first he tried to maintain a measure of control over his own life by slipping food and clothing. As long as he did this, he discovered, he was at the mercy of his captors. When he accepted the fact that he had no control at all, however, when he embraced his own vulnerability and gave himself over entirely to God's keeping come life or death, his jailers no longer had power over him. He was free; he became the powerful, his captors the powerless.

Didn't Jesus teach that strength lies in turning the other cheek, in loving enemies, in praying for those who misuse us? Isn't that the way he lived–not as conquering hero but as suffering servant? Don't misunderstand his power. If we do, we misunderstand him. We experience the Mighty God in our humility and weakness, not in our strength.

Notice also that this might is demonstrated, not in weapons, but in influence. There should be no doubt about which is stronger. We all know that the War Between the States ended the practice of slavery in this country. This social change was achieved by force. It came at a cost of hundreds of thousands of lives and untold suffering. One group in America, though, ended the practice of slavery eighty years earlier with no hostility and no bloodshed.

In the mid-1700s John Woolman, a Quaker, worked as a clerk. In this capacity one of his assignments was to write a bill of sale for a black female slave. He did so with great pangs of conscience, but vowed never to be a party to such a transaction again. Often when asked to write wills, he would handle everything except the clause about slaves. More than once, while explaining his convictions, he prompted the voluntary emancipation of slaves.

Woolman became a successful merchant, but not wanting to be "encumbered" with business, he supported his family by farming so that during certain seasons he could travel through the colonies to plead with Quakers to release their slaves. He purchased hundreds of slaves and gave them their freedom. He refused to use sugar or molasses because they were produced by slave labor. He began wearing unbleached muslin suits because dye for coloring suits was extracted from indigo, and indigo was raised by slave labor. Foolish? Eccentric? Perhaps, but after 1787 no American Quaker owned a slave.

Life is changed permanently for good, not by a right created by might, but by a might created by right. We discover that kind of might in the Mighty God in the manger. He does not force us to follow him; does not force the world to be his. He wins followers through influence, demonstrates power through humility, and shows his way through love. Therefore, we call him Mighty God.

How can a humble and loving God who works without force change the world? Wouldn't it be better if the God of might, the God who indeed is omnipotent, were to come with power and glory and exert divine will? Wouldn't it be better if this God were to demonstrate power in an unmistakable display, eliminate pain and suffering, and make divine purposes work? Can we trust this kind of God?

The fact is that God did not choose to show might in the way we think is right. In love, humility, and hope we see God's might. There is political might and spiritual might. One will pass away; one will endure.

Day Five
A Name for the Child:
"Everlasting Father"

It seems odd to approach the manger in Bethlehem, look at the child lying there, and call him "Father." The title "father" or "mother" belongs to an adult who has become a parent, not to a child. Even for this child, unique among all the babies that have ever been born, the name has a strange sound. We do not call Jesus "Father." We have conditioned ourselves to speak of God as Father, Son, and Holy Spirit, and we think "This child is the Son, the 'second person of the Godhead.' "

Well, that is just one way that theology can sometimes get in the way and cloud our understanding. Make no mistake, this child is God! This child is God's humanity and self-revelation showing who God is. The name "Father" is altogether appropriate for this baby for two reasons. First, the term "Father" is perhaps the best definition of God that we have. Second, this child has created a family—a universal, eternal family of believers. "Everlasting Father" is a good name for the baby of Bethlehem.

If we can appreciate this concept of Christ as "Father," we can understand a lot of things about this child, and, at the same time, understand a lot of things about ourselves. Perhaps this name says as much about us as it does about the child. The name "Father" says something about belonging. If we call God in Christ "Father," we are confessing that we are God's children. To belong, to live in an indissoluble relationship, is the most basic of all human needs. A young man who had spent two years in prison went to see his minister upon his release. While he was cut off from them, he had come to appreciate the blessings of family, friends, and society. He said, "I do not want much in life. I only want to belong again."

Belonging, living in a relationship with others to whom we are responsible and from whom we receive strength and support, enables us to deal with the question, "Who am I?" The absence of a feeling of belonging and identity generates many personal problems. If a person does not know who he is or if she doesn't feel secure in belonging to someone, that person cannot become a mature human being. Many studies document the so-called "identity crisis" as the root of alcoholism, drug addiction, teenage rebellion, and marriage and family breakup. The feeling that one does not belong is a missing link in personal emotional development.

To call God in Christ "Father" is to address this fundamental need of belonging. This is not an abstract term. It does not just describe one aspect of God, it is a relational term. You cannot call God "Father" without thereby confessing that you are a son or daughter. The child whose birth we celebrate at Christmas teaches us to say, "God is my Father! I am God's child. I bear an honorable and eternal name." Isn't that what the Christian gospel strives to communicate—that God is our "Everlasting Father" and every other human being on planet earth is our brother or sister?

This concept of "Father" represents the hope of the ages. Jesus was certainly not the first teacher to use the name "Father" in reference to God, nor were the Jewish people in their use of the term. The designation "Father" occurs in the literature of almost all early religions. Primitive tribes spoke of their local deities as "Father." Homer wrote about a "father of men and gods." This way of imagining God evolved naturally. In early societies the male parent was in a position of authority; he was lord of the family or clan. The idea of "Father" addressed to one's god had in it the hope for protection, affection, and provision. Addressing the tribal god as "Father" was an effort to secure his good favor, safety, and identity.

In the Christ child we affirm that the true God and "Everlasting Father" has come. We do not have to seek or appease god. God seeks us, breaks through our defenses, offers more than protection, gives everlasting love, and makes us part of God's divine life. If we accept this relationship, a bond is established that is unbreakable. We know who we are. We know what we are to become, for the name "Everlasting Father" does not mean simply that we belong but also that we receive direction and discipline.

From Bedlam to Bethlehem

I like folktales because they reveal traits and aspirations that are common to all persons. An old Norwegian tale indicates our need for help in knowing ourselves. A boy walking in the woods found an egg in a nest, took it home, and placed it with the eggs under a goose. When the egg hatched, out came a freakish creature. Its feet seemed to be deformed— they were clawlike—and it stumbled as it tried to follow the little geese. Its beak was not flat; it was pointed and twisted. Instead of having a lovely cream-colored down, it was an ugly brown color. To top it off, this creature made a terrible squawking sound! It seemed to be a genetic freak— an ugly, disfigured misfit.

One day a giant eagle flew across the barnyard. The eagle swept lower and lower until the strange, awkward little bird on the ground lifted its head and pointed its crooked beak into the sky. Something within this misfit creature responded to the eagle soaring above. It stretched its wings and began to hobble across the yard. It flapped its wings harder and harder until the wind picked him up and carried it into the sky. No longer was the bird an ugly, helpless freak; with its own, it was a majestic creature.

In the Christ child I see someone who comes to tell us that we belong and to inspire us to be who we are intended to be. He touches a yearning—a yearning to be accepted, to grow, to become. This world, like the barnyard for the young eagle, cannot satisfy us. As Augustine said, "Our souls are restless until they find rest in God." Likewise, our activities are meaningless until they are directed.

So, as loving "Everlasting Father," this child points us to the way by which our spirits can soar. He directs us to the obvious: Do the will of your Father; be perfect as your Father is perfect; forgive as your Father forgives; love your enemies and you will be called "sons of your Father;" go, and make disciples of all nations; live in trust, for no sparrow falls to the ground without your Father's knowledge; feed the hungry, give drink to the thirsty, welcome the stranger, clothe the naked, visit the sick, go to those in prison, and you will be called blessed (happy).

Being a child of God requires that in every experience we are pointed toward growth. God cares about our development. We belong and receive needed direction and discipline. We discover what security really is, for this relationship will not be terminated. As Paul indicates in his Galatian letter, we are no longer heirs, we are children forever (4:1).

Part of our trouble in speaking of God as Father lies in the fact that we tend to think in terms of earthly fathers. Every father I know is imperfect, but this Father is perfect. We must take into the word all that we long for–a permanent relationship, lasting security, sufficient strength —and we say that this Father provides all those things. Isaiah calls him "Everlasting Father," a Father forever, a Father eternally. This means that our Father will not allow our relationship with him to end. We do not fall from his care or stray from his concern. As Jesus told us in his story of the lost son, this Father will go to any length to win us back, and waits always to receive us.

What a beautiful name: Everlasting Father! What a profound concept: a lasting relationship that leads us to our true selves! It takes time to appreciate this. You can't rush it. Christmas, with all its mystery and wonder, is a good time to try to take it in, but we need the experiences of life to begin to understand it.

A visitor coming for the first time to the Grand Canyon found an old man who had spent many years at the canyon and asked which trips he should take to see the most of this great sight. The wise old man told him if he really wanted to see the canyon, he should not take any trips at all. Instead, he should come out early in the morning and take a seat on the rim, sit there and watch the morning pass into noontime and the noontime into afternoon, with the everchanging colors gleaming across the timeless stones. The old man then advised the visitor to get a quick supper and hurry back to watch the purple twilight come over the vast abyss. The old man said that if one runs around, he merely wears himself out and misses the greatness and beauty of it all.

We tend to banter the word "Father" around lightly and spend ourselves and our time looking for some new experience or way of looking at ourselves. All the while our "Everlasting Father" is in the shadows keeping watch over his own. Live, watch, and wait. We can discover the greatness and beauty of this relationship when we call the Christ child "Everlasting Father."

Day Six
A Name for the Child:
"Prince of Peace"

"For a child has been born for us, a son is given to us . . . and he is named 'Wonderful Counselor, Mighty God, Everlasting Father, Prince of Peace.' " So wrote Isaiah more than 700 years before the birth of the Christ child. The centuries have not dimmed the hope voiced by the prophet long ago. Isaiah's names for the child of Bethlehem still evoke powerful feelings.

We, too, need an understanding and compassionate "Counselor," a "Mighty God" who shares divine strength through love and grace, an "Everlasting Father" who includes each of us in the family, a "Prince of Peace" who heals our troubled hearts and troubled world. Each of these names has immense value.

This year we come again to the manger to see the child. Perhaps hesitatingly, but very hopefully, we call him "Prince of Peace." This name touches a fundamental need in every person's life, the need for peace of mind and peace of heart. This need is evident in the way we pursue almost any technique or program that promises to still the unrest that haunts us. Beneath the placid exteriors of our lives lies a battleground of emotions. Fear, tension, and anxiety create for many persons a situation like that of the man of whom it was said, "He is not so much a personality as a civil war."

All of us perk up when we hear of a new plan for dealing with worry, coping with frustration, or discovering peace of mind. We desperately desire peace, for the absence of peace prevents us from being ourselves. Persons who lack peace within are at odds with others. They will say things they do not mean and hurt those whom they love most. They will deal with conflict with methods of which they do not entirely approve and gradually become more and more strangers to themselves. All of us would agree: we need and desire peace within ourselves so that we can truly be ourselves.

A Name for the Child: "Prince of Peace"

What do we mean by peace? What kind of peace do we desire? Unfortunately, various spurious types of peace make their appeal. One type is the apparent peace of comfort. With your imagination visualize what is assumed to be the ideal family scene. The day's activities have ended; there is time for relaxation. Persons in this family are neither disturbed by serious problems nor worried about financial insecurity. They have a contented feeling of physical and mental well-being. We might be quick to label this situation an atmosphere of peace, a scene suitable for a Christmas card. In our affluent society, comfortable surroundings are commonplace; yet, lives are more deeply affected by boredom and emptiness than ever before. Where is the peace that we would expect from our abundance?

Another false peace is the peace of compromise. If personal peace is threatened by an internal conflict of ideals, the logical approach is to eliminate the conflict. Rid yourself of temptation by yielding to it. Don't be bothered by standards that you think are arbitrary. Set your own pace. Do your own thing. Despite the modern ring of such statements, this attitude has a long history. The Greek philosopher Epicurus conceived of peace as the "absence of pain in the body or a trouble in the mind." His formula for peace, therefore, was detachment, insulation against life. Epicurus sought a life that was self-contained, independent of the feelings, needs, and demands of others.

Many people will settle for a peace that comes through the enjoyment of things and pleasures. Others will try to content themselves with the superficial tranquility that arises from a retreat from challenge and involvement with others. These approaches to peace are essentially negative, however. They fall far short of the peace that comes through abundant living and an enthusiastic acceptance of life with all of its problems and possibilities. Personal peace is a spiritual matter that cannot be resolved with material acquisitions.

The relatives of an eccentric man assembled after his death to hear his last will and testament. He had not been wealthy, and most of his family members thought it strange that they would be summoned. They wondered what he had to leave them that would be of any value. They soon found out as the will was read:

> To my brother Alex I leave my sense of humor, inasmuch as he has never cracked a smile in his life. . . . To my cousin Sara I leave my optimism to mitigate her habitual gloomy and pessimistic view of things. . . . To my nephew Richard I leave my standard of values, in the hope that it may help him to learn that a man's life does not consist in the abundance of his possessions.

On it went, conveying a legacy of spiritual qualities, none of which was negotiable in terms of cash, but all of genuine worth in terms of living.

The Prince of Peace might challenge our usual expectations. The peace of God is different from the peace of the world, so we must ask about the kind of peace we desire. To know God's peace is to surrender our pet notions and learn from what God has shown us in Jesus Christ. While the general human understanding of peace is an absence of conflict and pain, and the general approach to peace is negative, the peace we find in Christ is positive.

The biblical concept of peace is based on the Hebrew word *shalom* and the Greek word *eirene*. *Shalom* means "everything that makes for a person's highest good," or everything that contributes to giving life security and meaning and brings about inner harmony. *Eirene* refers to the serenity that comes through righteousness and a perfection of relationship, specifically the relationship between God and humans. Together these words give us an understanding of peace that describes the totality of a life in which one is related to others and to God.

This peace has been created by God's reconciling work in Jesus Christ. As Paul said in his Ephesian letter, "he is our peace." He has reconciled us to God and to each other, having "broken down the dividing wall" (2:14). Christ has made peace by destroying all the barriers that prevent peace. Christian peace arises from harmony with God and with God's will. This is the basis for the proclamation of the angels: "And on earth peace among those whom he favors" (Luke 2:14). This possibility could be announced because in Christ, God demonstrated God's attitude toward creation. This attitude is one of involvement and reconciliation. We can make this claim because God has come to be among us. One name of the child was to be Immanuel, which means "God with us" (Matt 1:23). If we could get behind the glitter and the trappings of the season, we would find this truth to be the key to the celebration of Christmas. God is with us and for us.

God is with us and in us, creating peace. The peace that comes to us in Christ is an active force within us that enables us to overcome all the things that work against peace. Many things pull and divide our lives in today's culture; Christ offers the grace to restore that which is divided.

Christ's peace overcomes our inner division. Jesus said, "If a house is divided against itself, that house will not be able to stand" (Mark 3:25). This comment applies directly to the divided soul and speaks to a pervasive problem in modern life. It has been pointed out that "a person has as many different selves as there are distinct groups of persons about whose opinion he cares." We unconsciously allow the expectations of others to force us to maintain an external social front that might not reflect our true personality. If we are not certain about the self at the center, we will try to conceal our emptiness. Image and reputation take on an importance all out of proper proportion. Our desire to be loved and respected becomes more significant to us than honesty with ourselves. This is inner division.

Christ delivers us from the strain of pretense. He calls us to accept the priority of God's kingdom and righteousness and to find the true self of which we can be unashamed. Thus, we come to have a soundness at the core of our being that shatters divisive emotions. We cannot have peace until we know and receive this inner soundness, and with it a peace that cannot be shaken.

The peace of Christ also overcomes the guilt that is so destructive in our lives and relationships. We are slow to recognize the harmful effects of guilt, the false guilt that arises from the unrealistic expectations and judgmental statements of others and the true guilt that emerges from our awareness that we are not what we should be. Not recognizing or accepting our guilt, we try to repress it in busyness or in pleasure. Christ offers the only outlet for guilt: forgiveness. He enables us to own up to our faults and thus disown them, to confess our sins so that they cease to be ours.

The peace of Christ helps us to handle another great nemesis to personal peace: the threat of fear. We have inner tension because we are afraid, afraid of disappointment and failure, afraid of illness, afraid of the future. This fear often drives us to despair.

A succession of reverses once threw Martin Luther into a prolonged mood of depression. At length his wife Katie came to his rescue. One morning she appeared at the breakfast table dressed in black. Luther looked up in amazement. "Who is dead?" he asked. Katie replied, "Do you not know? God is dead." Luther reproved her for her blasphemy. Sharply he asked, "How can God be dead? He is eternal." "Yes," she answered, "but from the way you are cast down, one would think that God must be dead."[1] Luther was trapped by his own statement and recognized his own lack of trust.

Obviously, we cannot always easily deal with our fears nor quickly put aside our apprehensions, but the awareness that God is with us can help us to cope. In the eighth chapter of the book of Romans, Paul surveys all the enemies of peace, all the forces that challenge personal well-being, and he declares that nothing can separate us from God's love in Jesus Christ. "If God is for us," he asks, "Who is against us? He who did not spare his own Son but gave him up for us all, will he not also give us all things with him?" (8:31-32, RSV)

The Prince of Peace becomes our peace. He is peace; he brings peace. He overcomes every destructive force, brings us into harmony with the will of God, and thus creates harmony within our lives. He overcomes every destructive force within our lives. The anticipation of the prophet melts into the angelic announcement: "Glory to God in the highest heaven, and on earth peace among those whom he favors!"

Day Seven
The Savior of the World

To Joseph the angel said of the child that Mary would bear: "You are to name him Jesus, for he will save his people from their sins." (Matt 1:21)

When the day came and the baby arrived, an angel announced, "To you is born this day in the city of David a Savior, who is the Messiah, the Lord."
—(Luke 2:11)

Jesus is a Greek name based on the Hebrew name Joshua, which means "God saves." In the day of Joseph and Mary it was a common name. A lot of Jewish babies were called Jesus, because the name referred to the hope of God's redemption. Savior is another matter, however. Savior was a title normally reserved for successful military leaders or important government officials. It referred to one who brought deliverance or established freedom. No baby would be called Savior.

All the more baffling is the message of the angel: "To you is born . . . a Savior." Actually, Jesus is called Savior in only one other place in the Gospels. Yet how easily you and I look at the baby in the Christmas family and call him Savior! We speak of him as our "personal Savior." We call him "Savior of the world." We sing "Savior, Like a Shepherd Lead Us," "Jesus, Savior, Pilot Me," and "What a Wonderful Savior." How do we so readily call this child Savior?

To understand the idea of a savior, we have to say what we mean by salvation. In the work of salvation, in what the Christ child came to reveal and grew up to accomplish, the name Savior takes meaning. In that work of salvation we discover what is unique about the child in the manger. The angels announced it. Have we paid attention?

Salvation has decisive importance for the Christian faith. It is central to faith itself. Salvation is the work of God whereby a person is delivered from the sinful selfhood into newness and fullness of life. It is transformation by which a person is set free from sin and death. It is a liberation. One is "saved from" some things, but Christian salvation is much more than a negative experience. It is also positive; we are "saved to" a life like God's life. We receive salvation; we cannot create it. Not only are we liberated; we are changed. We grow toward the full maturity that God intends for each of us. Salvation, then, is a comprehensive word signifying what life is all about.

Salvation comes from outside us. We accept it. Apart from God's revelation we cannot talk about salvation. Indeed, apart from God's revelation we would not even know that salvation were necessary or possible. What does the child of Bethlehem have to do with this process called salvation? Why do we call him Savior? In this baby God has revealed God's self, will, way, and purpose. Such ideas are better told with story than with argument. The following story tells about God's intervention in Christ "from the point of view of the angels in heaven.

Once upon a time a very young angel was being shown round the splendors and glories of all the created order by a senior and experienced angel. Finally he was shown the galaxy of which our planetary system is but a small part. As the two of them drew near to the star that we call our sun and to its circling planets, the senior angel pointed to a small and rather insignificant sphere turning very slowly on its axis and said,

"I want you to watch that one particularly," said the senior angel, pointing with his finger.

"Well, it looks very small and rather dirty to me," said the little angel. "What's special about that one?"

"That," replied his senior solemnly, "is the Visited Planet."

"Visited?" said the little one. "You don't mean visited by Him, do you?"

"Indeed I do. That ball, which I have no doubt looks to you small and insignificant and not perhaps overclean, has been visited by our young Prince of Glory." And at these words he bowed his head reverently.

"But how?" queried the younger one. "Do you mean that our great and glorious Prince, with all these wonders and splendors of His creation, and millions more that I'm sure I haven't seen yet, went down in person to this fifth-rate little ball? Why should He do a thing like that?"

"It isn't for us," said his senior, a little stiffly, "to question His why's, except that I must point out to you that He is not impressed by size and numbers as you seem to be. But that He really went I know, and all of us in Heaven who know anything know that. As to why He became one of them . . . How else do you suppose could He visit them?"

The little angel's face wrinkled in disgust. "Do you mean to tell me," he said, "that He stooped so low as to become one of those creeping, crawling creatures of that floating ball?"

"I do, and I don't think He would like you to call them 'creeping, crawling creatures' in that tone of voice. For, strange as it may seem to us, He loves them. He went down to visit them to lift them up to become like Him." The little angel looked blank. Such a thought was almost beyond his comprehension.

God became one of us. Humans, as sinful and helpless as we are, are not beyond the concern and grace of God. In fact, humanity and its tiny planet, soiled and marred as they both are with the ugliness and pain brought on by rebellion and strife, hatred and cruelty, have become not "off limits" to the concern of the Eternal God but the very center of God's grace and the object of divine love. In Jesus God came to be Savior.

In order to be the Savior, God chose to become a human being, to come as a flesh-and-blood baby. Why as a baby? Why as one of us? God could have remained remote from us and given us instructions as to how to be saved. God could have left a prescription or a "do-it-yourself" manual for bringing about personal transformation. Other philosophies and religions have taken that approach. Rather, God chose to come as one of us to guide us, to show us the way, to encourage us along the way we should go, to love us into becoming like Christlike. That is astounding! Persons might see the need for and desire salvation, but without the personal love and encouragement they remain helpless.

Anne Morrow was shy and delicate—butterfly-like, not dull or stupid or incompetent, just a quiet specimen of timidity. Her dad was an ambassador to Mexico. There she met an adventurous young fellow who visited south of the border for the U.S. State Department. He flew from place to place promoting aviation. Everywhere he went he drew crowds. He had just won $40,000 for being the first person to fly across the Atlantic. The dashing pilot and the shy girl fell deeply in love.

When she became Mrs. Charles Lindberg, Anne could have lost her own personality. Her husband was a national hero, always in the limelight. Anne Morrow Lindberg could have become a resentful recluse, a nameless face in a crowd of admirers. Instead, she became one of America's most popular authors. Her own gifts blossomed. Why and how? Because she loved and was loved.

I know of nothing that inspires us to accept salvation as powerfully as the presence and encouragement of Jesus Christ. Some people seek salvation out of fear; they're afraid of what might happen if they are not "saved." Those people almost never enjoy their salvation; they're always worrying about losing it. Some seek salvation because they're told they should be saved; those people rarely grow in their experience. For them salvation is static; it is a thing to be collected. Others seek salvation because they have seen the Savior and long to be like him, because daily they hear his encouragement and feel his power. What unbelievable fulfillment lies ahead for them!

At Christmastime think of that to which the child saves us. The Savior invites us to be saved in order to become like him. He urges us to be fully human as he was fully human, to be fully alive as he was fully alive, to be fully loving as he was fully loving, to be fully committed to the will of God as he was fully committed to the will of God.

Note

[1]Cited by Leonard Griffith, *The Eternal Legacy* (New York: Harper & Row, Publishers, 1963) 132.

The Third
Week of Advent

A Season for Giving

Day One
It Is also Blessed to Receive

Thanks be to God for his indescribable gift! (2 Cor 9:15)

A lot of gift-giving is taking place right now. Making gifts to loved ones and exchanging gifts with friends are an integral part of our celebration of Christmas. Some persons are adept at gift-giving. They seem almost to know instinctively what gift is most appropriate for the person they have in mind. They show care in selecting it and take pains to wrap it attractively. Giving is an art. Not everyone is good at it, but it remains, especially at this particular time, something important to all of us.

Giving has two sides. Not only must a gift be given; it must be received. In fact, a gift is not a gift unless it is received, and not everyone is good at receiving. Perhaps we need to concentrate on this other side of giving. We tend to discount the significance of receiving. We repeat the statement of Jesus, "It is more blessed to give than to receive" (Acts 20:35) and focus primarily on what we can give at Christmastime. It is also blessed to receive, however.

During this season we focus on the greatest gift that has ever been made—the gift that God has made of himself in Jesus Christ. It is a truly a gift—a unique gift, a living gift, and, if you will, a free gift. It is a unique gift, because no one but God could give it. It is a living gift, because we cannot open it, look at it, and put it aside. Rather, it is a life that enables us to rise above our failings, rebellion, and weaknesses. It is a free gift; it has no conditions and will not be recalled.

What other gift can measure up to this one? When Paul pondered the meaning of God's gracious self-giving he exulted, "Thanks be to God for his indescribable gift!" We should properly call attention to this gift, proclaim it, and try to understand what it means. Yet, we should not stop with praising the gift but go on to receive it. We should not place it on an ecclesiastical shelf as something to bring out and dust off at Christmas time. We must gratefully receive this gift. About God's gift in Jesus Christ John said, "To all who received him, who believed in his name, he gave power to become children of God" (1:12).

Do not underestimate the value of receiving. The giving of gifts is difficult, but receiving a gift can also be difficult. Not being able to receive might be more tragic than not being able to give. What is involved in receiving a gift?

First, you just receive it. You accept it for what it is. Sounds easy, doesn't it? It's not. Some persons get a Christmas card and rush to mail one to the sender. For some persons, getting an unexpected present without having an opportunity to reciprocate can be a terrible experience. In response to a surprise gift, they say, "You shouldn't have . . ." To a sincere and well-intentioned compliment, they reply, "You don't really mean that."

According to this mind-set, everything requires some kind of repayment. Maybe our society is so manipulative and filled with gifts that come with strings attached that peace of mind necessitates that all giving be balanced out. What does that do for a gift or the giver of a gift? It makes a gift a problem. Therefore, I say that the act of receiving means that we just receive what is given.

Just as giving that is done well requires more than the random choice of something to give, so receiving that is done well requires more than the random choice of something to give and passive acceptance.

To receive is also to share. Think of some valuable gift that you have received. It was probably something that you were able to share, something that brought joy both to you and someone else. That's part of the miracle of giving.

Leo Buscaglia tells about an extended visit to Hong Kong. He wasn't in the city long before he began to go every evening to Star Ferry, there to sit and watch commuters on their way home, and to enjoy the changing colors of the harbor at dusk. One evening he noticed a young man on the end of the bench. He was engrossed in a book and seemed oblivious to the noisy passersby and the deepening sunset. Every evening thereafter Buscaglia found the young man at the same spot, head bowed over the book. One night he looked up and asked, "Can you help me say this word?" Buscaglia saw that the book was an English-Chinese dictionary. As he helped the young Chinese with pronunciations, the new friend volunteered that his name was Wong and that he was trying to teach himself English so that he could get a good job and make a better life for himself and his family.

For several nights Buscaglia met Wong. He taught Wong conversational English; Wong became his tour guide around Hong Kong. Wong's story came out. He was the eldest son in a large family, the only family member working. His English-Chinese dictionary was his only hope out of a desperate situation. Buscaglia was impressed. Before leaving Hong Kong, he paid the modest tuition for Wong to attend an English language school.

Two years later, back in the U.S., Buscaglia received a note from Wong. He was speaking English well. He had found a better job, and his family had moved to better quarters. Enclosed in the letter was a bank note to repay what Wong saw as a debt. Buscaglia returned the money with these instructions: "Wong, please take this money down to the Star Ferry, and when you find a young man sitting there under a street lamp, trying to learn English from a dictionary, give him the money from both of us, with love."[1]

A genuine gift, a gift that suits our needs, a gift that comes with our best interests at heart, will always, if properly received, make of us larger persons. Isn't that what God's gift does? Receiving it enables us to become children of God. Receiving the gift means receiving God, taking on God's nature, becoming infinitely greater than we are. It means that we accept a relationship and a fellowship. We accept membership in a family. There we share the gift and the life and the joy. We pass on the gift, and, as we do, the gift multiplies in value to us.

The act of receiving requires that we actually receive a gift. It means that we share something with the giver and with others. It also binds us to the giver. I do not mean to contradict what I said earlier, that a gift made in genuine love has no strings attached. A real gift does not force anything, but a gift that is given and received in love binds the giver and the recipient.

Again, rummage mentally through the things you treasure as your most valuable gifts. You will probably come up with a hand-made card from your child or some item from your spouse. You will recall the occasion when the gift was made, but beyond the occasion you will think of the person. The gift becomes a symbol of the bond between you and that person.

Because of the bond between the giver and receiver, the church embraces Christmas with fervor. Churches do not try to impress anybody by decorating the sanctuary and scheduling special services. They are looking again at the gift God has made to us; the gift of love, life, hope, and joy; the gift that, as John tells us, makes the difference between light and darkness, life and death. Christians rejoice again to see the gift as meaningful and as appealing as ever. We try to receive it, or to receive more of it. Not one of us has yet received all that it can be for us.

Several years ago after one of our larger family Christmas gatherings, after aunts and uncles, cousins, nieces and nephews had all exchanged and opened small gifts, there was one present still under the tree. We did not know who had placed it there, but the card on top indicated that it was for an aunt who was not able to come. One of her sisters took the present home, saying she would pass it on at the first opportunity. The present was placed on a table in the guest bedroom, and there it stayed. On a visit to that home the next summer I spotted the present. The colorfully-wrapped package seemed terribly out of place on a warm June day. As I looked at the present, however, I thought, "This gift was not really a gift. Someone chose it and tried to give it, but it was never received."

How tragic that the greatest of all gifts, for so many persons, goes unreceived! While we think during the next few days about what we shall give, let us give some consideration to and preparation for what we shall receive.

Day Two
A Time for Giving

When they saw that the star had stopped, they were overwhelmed. On enter-ing the house, they saw the child with Mary his mother; and they knelt down and paid him homage. Then, opening their treasure chests, they offered him gifts of gold, frankincense, and myrrh.

—(Matt 2:10-11)

Each year during the Christmas season a delightful little story, "The Grinch Who Stole Christmas," by Dr. Seuss is televised. The Grinch was a surly character who was jeal-ous of the residents of Whoville. He was especially resentful of the joy and laughter they shared at Christmas. The Grinch reasoned that gifts and decorations made the people of Whoville happy, so he decided to "steal" Christmas. He carried away all the trees and trimmings, the gifts, and the food that had been prepared for the celebration—every trace of Christmas.

When Christmas morning dawned, the Grinch looked down on the village, expecting to see the people bowed in sadness, but to his amazement there were no tears. The people came out of their houses, stood hand in hand in the snow, and began to sing the joyful songs of Christmas. The Grinch had taken only the external gifts from Whoville.

No one can take away the gift of a joyful heart. It is a gift of God in Jesus. Christmas is a time for giving and receiving. It is a time for celebrating the greatest gift that has ever been given: God's gift of Jesus Christ. What kind of gift has God given? We must see this gift very clearly, for it is a personal gift for each of us.

Notice how Matthew describes this gift. Joseph, a young car-penter of Nazareth, tossed fitfully in his sleep. He was deeply disturbed because Mary, his fiancée, was expecting a child. Since he knew the child was not his, Joseph had to make a terrible deci-sion. He would have to divorce her. In that day, an engagement could be broken only by a formal divorce. Joseph felt the sting of disappointment and anger. In a dream, however, he saw an angel. The angel said,

> Joseph, son of David, do not be afraid to take Mary as your wife, for the child conceived in her is from the Holy Spirit. She will bear a son, and you are to name him Jesus, for he will save his people from their sins (1:20-21).

This angelic message rescued Joseph from despair and gave him a new sense of direction. Also it described, in stark simplicity, the gift God was preparing not only for Joseph and Mary but for all people: the gift of salvation. "He shall save his people from their sins."

We should be reminded of God's gift each time we hear the name "Jesus," for "Jesus" means "YAHWEH is salvation." This is the central meaning of the Christian gospel: Jesus has come to bring salvation. What does the gift of salvation mean in our lives? What effect does it have?

The Bible does not gloss over the problem of human existence; the problem is sin, for sin separates us from God and humans from his or her true existence. Sin is the source of our misery and heartache; it is the pain that cuts deep into our lives. Jesus has the power to save us from our sins, however!

Specifically, how does the salvation of God help us to overcome the problem of sin in our lives? First, it releases us from the burden of guilt. Guilt is self-judgment. It is the awareness that our lives are much less than they ought to be. Guilt arouses remorse. It diverts our attention from others to ourselves, for we constantly worry about what might be wrong with us. The cure for guilt is not just remorse but a change of heart, a new attitude. Salvation eliminates the sense of guilt and delivers a person from worry and self-punishment.

Second, the salvation of Jesus satisfies our need for dependence. We try to project our image of self-sufficiency, but behind the bravado, we know keenly that we are "dependent" creatures. We need something sturdy and unshakable on which to depend. Christmas reminds us that "something" is really "someone"– someone who is a living friend, someone who beckons to us,

"Come to me, all you that are weary and are carrying heavy burdens, and I will give you rest" (Matt 11:28).

I once spent several months plowing through some of the writings of an influential German theologian named Friedrich Schleiermacher. Schleiermacher defined Christian faith as a "feeling of absolute dependence." When we experience salvation, we shift our dependence from ourselves and our things to God.

Third, salvation has something to do with our helplessness. We sometimes come to the point where we feel absolutely helpless to alter a bad situation. We ask whether we are not simply pawns of fate. We want to escape. Salvation gives us the power to overcome, however, for we no longer trust ourselves but God.

To say that Jesus "saves us from our sins" means that he delivers us from guilt, self-dependence, and helplessness by the gift of himself to us. We are given his strength, his power, his way, for he comes to live in us. His life becomes our life.

Dr. Ernest Gordon, chaplain of Princeton University, was a prisoner of the Japanese in Thailand during World War II. He was placed in the camp on which the book and movie *The Bridge over the River Kwai* were based. Gordon wrote a book entitled *Through the Valley of the Kwai* in which he reflected on the difference between two Christmas seasons spent in the prison. In 1942 the camp was dirty, and no one cared. In 1943 a big, strong prisoner who had been taking care of his buddy was noticed to be withering away. He was giving nearly all the food he received to his fellow prisoner, who was quite sick. Finally the soldier who had been well died, and the sick man got well.

The story of the man who had sacrificed his life for his buddy went throughout the camp. Men began to clean up and take new hope. They recalled Bible verses and held discussions about Christianity and the Bible. A different attitude and atmosphere came over the entire camp. Dr. Gordon called it "the miracle of Kwai." The difference between Christmas 1942 and Christmas 1943 was made by a man with a Christlike spirit—a spirit of giving.

This is God's gift to us at Christmas—salvation, new life. Paul stated it well in Romans: "For the wages of sin is death, but the free gift of God is eternal life in Christ Jesus our Lord" (6:23).

72

Christmas is a time for giving and receiving, but have you ever noticed that receiving stimulates a desire to give? Not only do we receive a gift from God, but we bring gifts to God. Let me show you what I mean by pointing to the Christmas story.

Matthew tells about wise men or magi—mysterious visitors from the East—who came to Bethlehem in search of Jesus. When they found Joseph, Mary, and the baby, "they knelt down and paid him homage." Then they presented their gifts. According to legend, Caspar brought gold, a gift of wealth and substance; Melchior brought frankincense, which, because it is a fragrance, represents man's inner treasure of influence and thought that must be given to Christ; and Balthazzar brought myrrh, a precious gift fit only for a king.

Notice carefully the significance of these gifts. The kingship of Jesus Christ is the theme of Matthew's gospel. The gifts of the magi reflected an awareness of Jesus' kingship over life and property. The gifts were material. In a sense, they were financial gifts. Have we recognized the kingship of Christ over life? Have we given the gift of personal, material, and financial stewardship? To say that we serve Christ and to withhold these gifts from him is a shabby kind of discipleship.

Luke tells about shepherds who came to see the baby Jesus. We would expect an emphasis on shepherds because one of Luke's primary interests was to show that the gospel is for common people, not merely the mighty. Shepherds were not highly regarded by the orthodox religious people of that day. Their flocks made constant demands on them, they were not able to attend regular times of worship and prayer in the synagogues, and they could not observe the handwashings and rules and regulations. But to this group—spurned by organized religion—the angel came to proclaim news of Jesus' birth. The shepherds traveled to Bethlehem and saw the child. They were gripped by the awesome display of God's power. They gave the Christ child the only thing they had to give: their faith. Have you given your faith to God in response to God's gift to you?

Two other characters in the Christmas story gave precious gifts: Mary and Joseph. They gave their lives. They surrendered the plans they had made for themselves to carry out God's will and be parents of God's son. After all, is that not what is ultimately required—the gift of life to the one who has given us life?

Yes, this is a time for giving and receiving. We receive God's gift by giving ourselves. A wonderful poem by Christina Rosetti describes the simple way we respond to God's love. God's gift awakens our desire to give, but

> What can I give Him, poor as I am?
> If I were a shepherd, I would bring a lamb.
> If I were a wise man, I would do my part.
> What can I give Him—give my heart.[2]

Giving and receiving cannot be separated. As we accept God's gift, we make to God the gift of ourselves.

Day Three
The Right Gift

The point is this: the one who sows sparingly will also reap sparingly, and the one who sows bountifully will also reap bountifully. Each of you must give as you have made up your mind, not reluctantly or under compulsion, for God loves a cheerful giver.

—(2 Cor 9:6-7)

Christmas is a season for giving. Unfortunately, a poor perspective on giving can lead to undue commercialization, and the pressure to exchange gifts as a matter of course can distort the whole purpose of giving. Still, there is something very precious in the impulse to give and to share. Giving is a vital part of our celebration of the coming of Jesus Christ.

Giving is associated with Christmas, because Christmas represents God's gift of God's self to us. What God did in becoming man can hardly be described other than as a gift of love and grace, as Paul recognized. In his letter to the Romans he referred to the new life brought by Jesus Christ as a "free gift of righteousness" (5:17). In 2 Corinthians he exclaimed, "Thanks be to God for his indescribable gift" (9:15).

We think about God's gift to us at Christmas, the greatest and most meaningful gift humanity has ever received. As we consider this gift, let us think about our own patterns of giving and receiving. Behind every gift lies a purpose or motive. This motive will have a significant bearing on what a gift will mean to the receiver. Despite the keen desire that we all have for gifts, we certainly want no gift that is not intended for us, and we want no gift that is granted in the wrong spirit. Such gifts are empty, even harmful.

Yet, much gift-giving is done for the wrong purpose. Sometimes gifts are made in the self-interest of the giver. Paul Tournier, in a thought- provoking little book entitled *The Meaning of Gifts,* cites this example:

> When husband and wife are in conflict, often we see them go to excess in spoiling the children, at times sharing foolishly-made

confidences in order to tie the children to them, all for the purpose of strengthening their side in the marriage conflict.[2]

Such gifts of overindulgence and permissiveness are in the interests, not of the receiver, but of the giver. Whenever a gift is presented on that basis, it has the negative effect of arousing distrust and confusion.

Closely related to the gift made in self-interest is the one that is conveyed for the purpose of domination or manipulation. How commonly we hear statements such as these: "Since I gave you that, now you must do this for me," and "I will give you this gift, if you will give me that." Genuine gifts do not come with strings attached. They cannot be used to negotiate for the allegiance or affection of the receiver.

Then there is the gift made on the basis of guilt. Someone hurts or offends another. That person cannot bring himself/herself to apologize or seek the forgiveness of the offended party, so he/she makes a gift, hoping the gift might accomplish what a verbal apology cannot.

Many other motives are woven into the fabric of our common life. We make gifts to demonstrate our generosity, or out of a sense of duty, or because others are watching. Judging our own purposes for giving is not always easy, for many times our motives are mixed. The real meaning of a gift will inevitably come back to the intent that it conveys, however, and there is but one standard by which to judge its value. What does the gift say of love? Love must be the basis—unconditional love that has no strings attached, freely given love that does not depend on reciprocation, caring love that seeks only the welfare of the receiver.

Seldom can you and I make our gifts from this kind of perspective. What we experience only occasionally approaches the perfect model of self-giving, but the Christmas gift of God to each of us comes from just such a love. God's giving of self in Jesus Christ was unforced. It grew out of no merit on our part and no hope of reward on God's part. It was given spontaneously as a result of God's loving nature. We cannot improve on John's simple observation: "For God so loved the world that he gave." (3:16).

Since we are unable to analyze or measure the mind of God, we can only offer praise for an inexpressible love and thanks for an inexpressible gift. However inexpressible the gift might be, it is not a gift that we cannot receive. In Jesus Christ the inexpressible becomes experiential. "When the fullness of time had come," Paul wrote to the Galatians, "God sent his Son." (4:4).

The way a Christmas gift is wrapped is important. The paper and the bow heighten the suspense and anticipation. A child will take a colorfully wrapped package from under a tree and yearn desperately to open it. God's gift to us could not have been presented more beautifully. We are enchanted by the sublime beauty with which Matthew and Luke tell the story. The scene of the manger, the child, the parents, the shepherds, and the magi is only the wrapping that invites us to open and receive the gift of love that God has conveyed. What is contained therein? The gift of God is one of self-commitment. We know very well that the greatest gift we can make to another person is the gift of ourselves. Things can never compensate for that gift of the self.

Perhaps you appreciate the letters and responses found in "Dear Abby." An interesting letter from a young father once appeared in that column. The man wanted his children to have the best and most he could give them, so in addition to his regular employment he had taken on two part-time jobs. Only by doing so could he earn enough to provide what he thought his family needed. He rarely saw his children, however, fortunately and he had the wisdom to realize that he was not really being a father to them; they needed him *with* them. Consequently, he dropped the part-time jobs and made room for family time.

The gift of oneself is indispensable, and that is precisely what God has given in Jesus Christ. "God was in Christ," and because of this reality, everything takes on a new meaning. God's gift is not an abstract thing. It is an intensely practical gift, relating to our needs and longings. Jesus once said,

> If you then, who are evil, know how to give good gifts to your chil-
> dren, how much more will your Father in heaven give good things to
> those who ask him! (Matt 5:11)

When we speak of God's self-giving, we are talking about a gift that is expressed in salvation, a gift that is expressed in peace, a gift that is expressed in freedom, a gift that is expressed in a rich and abundant life.

How valuable is the gift? To those persons content with the wrapping, it holds little significance. The worth or value of a gift will always be traced to the relationship between the giver and the receiver. The relationship will determine whatever appreciation or gratitude that might be felt. This leads us to the matter of receiving the gift. Some gifts are never truly received. We may take a gift, put it aside or add it to one's store of possessions, and fail to take note of the giver and his/her intentions. Such a gift has no purpose, not through the fault of the giver, but through the indifference of the receiver.

One truly sad thing about Christmas, I feel, is the indifference of so many toward God's inexpressible gift. Oh, everyone takes advantage of the holiday, and there is a general willingness to go through the motions of religious observance. When we consider the magnitude of what we celebrate, however, we have to wonder why there is not a deeper level of feeling behind our rituals. Maybe we are unable to receive the gift in all its fullness. More and more I am convinced that the meaning of faith for our lives is directly connected with our ability and willingness to receive what God has offered. If we receive the gift of God's self, if the gift becomes alive through a personal relationship, all the other things we desire such as security, inner peace, and direction come as by-products. If God is the center of our life, we lack nothing. We, in turn, realize that we have the resources in Christ to be the "cheer-ful giver."

Day Four
The Gifts of Christmas: Love

For God so loved the world that he gave his only Son, so that everyone who believes in him may not perish but may have eternal life.

—(John 3:16)

The gifts we present and the gifts we receive are expressions of the feeling and affection that we have for each other. Such expressions are necessary in our relationships. A gift brings delight both to the giver and the receiver. God has gifts for us all at Christmas, and it would be tragic for us not to accept them. The candles on the Advent wreath are sometimes seen as symbolic of four of God's gifts that are so precious in our experience: love, joy, peace, and hope.

Consider the gift of love. This gift is beautifully described in the fourth chapter of 1 John. There, with the exception of Paul's great hymn in 1 Corinthians 13, we find the most vivid dissertation on Christian love in the New Testament. John speaks of God's love from personal experience, a point he makes clear in the introduction to this work: "What we have heard, what we have seen with our eyes," he writes, "we declare to you" (1:1, 3). John had come into contact with love incarnate in his experience with Jesus Christ. He was an eyewitness, and he wanted his readers to share his marvelous discovery. His words have immense value.

The concept that God is love has decisive importance for religious experience. It cannot be overemphasized. Who God is and what God is like are persistent questions in religion. Every living religion and every growing faith engage in the quest for an adequate understanding of God. Only a dead religion or a dead faith ceases to raise this problem.

Faith cannot be content with the usual philosophical approaches. To say that God is a great Cause or Being or that God is Wisdom or Beauty simply does not satisfy the needs of faith. Such terms are cold and non-relational. John answers the questions with the simple affirmation: God is love. This is his candid and forthright approach to the essential nature of ultimate reality.

To accept that God is love requires one to believe that love governs all the other attributes of God. John bases his claim that God is love on the evidence of what God has done. Love defines the way that God relates to persons. The conviction that God is love can arise only from the personal experience of being loved and accepted by God.

John emphasizes that God's love is not an abstract emotion. It is revealed in events and revealed supremely in the Christ event: "God's love was revealed among us in this way: God sent his Son into the world" (4:9). John suggests that God's gift of his Son is the measure of God's love. Only in the light of that gift can we say that God is love, and only there do we discover the extent of that love. In Christ, God is present with all people.

We further comprehend the nature of this love when we realize that it is entirely unconditional and uncaused. Nothing on humanity's part stimulated its free expression: "Not that we loved God but that he loved us" (4:10). No matter how indifferent or even hostile a person feels toward God's love, divine love remains. It is a patient love, a suffering love, a self-giving love. Thus, it stands in contrast to any kind of human love. It transcends the limits of our understanding, resisting any type of comparison. God is perfect love, John would say. This is God's gift, a gift that conveys to us an understanding and knowledge of God.

This love transforms human life. No one who receives this gift can remain unaffected. John cites several changes that come about when a person accepts the gift of love. We enjoy helping our children make out their lists of things they would like for Christmas. If we were to compose a list of our own spiritual desires, the things John mentions would almost certainly be included.

We would certainly desire an assurance of our relationship with God. "Love is from God; everyone who loves is born of God and knows God" (4:7). Faith in God creates love in the life of the believer. So love becomes, not only a distinguishing mark of the Christian, but also the foundation of spiritual assurance. The deepest knowledge of God is never gained through thought or study or devotional discipline, however important those approaches might be. A few lines further on John says, "Those who abide in love abide in God, and God abides in them" (4:16).

Abiding in love poses a difficult problem, for love is to be directed not simply toward God but also toward people who are not easy to love. Christian love is not tested by the persons who return our love or by those who are good and kind toward us. No grace is required there. The test of our love comes in our attitudes and actions toward those who seem unlovable or unworthy. John says that God's love has overcome those very barriers and that as our love also transcends them and we become able to express it concretely, we discover the inward assurance that God is in our hearts.

God's gift of love gives us a sense of personal security also. John calls it a "boldness on the day of judgment" (4:17). For many persons, working out a concept of God is a discipline best left to the scholar. All of us have a concept of God, and the kind of view we have will inevitably determine how we see ourselves before God. If we see God as a vengeful deity, we will be overcome by a feeling of guilt and resist a close relationship with God. If we see God as a manager of the universe, we will fail to take our personal concerns to God. Therefore, we need to turn again and again to the fact that God is love, the loving Father who is infinitely more compassionate than any human father could ever be. God's love gives us the confidence that we are acceptable and accepted, that through our repentance, sin and guilt are removed.

Another welcome change is the elimination of fear: "There is no fear in love, but perfect love casts out fear" (4:18). To accept God's love is to be afraid of God no longer. Fear is a contradiction of love. Fear grows out of the belief that God is against us. In his acceptance of and identification with outcasts and sinners, Jesus demonstrated that God is love and grace.

God's love working within us to create a life of love enables us to find assurance and eradicate fear. This is not a seasonal gift that fades with time or that is put on the shelf and forgotten. Rather, love is a gift that remains to make life what it ought to be.

So far we have concentrated on the gift of love as it relates to the inner person. John was concerned with explaining that aspect of love, but he was no less concerned with its tangible expression in life. Throughout this passage we find practical exhortations: "Beloved, let us love one another" (4:7); "Beloved, since God loved us so much, we also ought to love one another" (4:11); "The commandment we have from him is this: those who love God must love their brothers and sisters also" (4:21). God's love inspires our love, and only as we receive God's gift of love can we truly love. The love of God in our hearts enables us to give ourselves and serve as can no other motivation.

An American journalist in China watched a Catholic sister cleansing the sores of a wounded soldier. "I wouldn't do that for a million dollars," he remarked. Without pausing in her work the sister quietly replied, "Neither would I." Only the love of God can call for the kind of noble service our world needs.

Whenever human love strives to imitate divine love, God is revealed. John says, "No one has ever seen God" (1 John 4:12), but there is a genuine indication of God's presence in the world when divine love is expressed through the Christian's life. Clement of Alexandria once said that the real Christian "practices being God."

In the Christ child, "God's love was revealed among us." To love is to bear God's image.

Day Five
The Gifts of Christmas: Joy

I have said these things to you so that my joy may be in you, and that your joy may be complete.

—(John 15:11)

A special gift of Christmas is the gift of joy. Some of us might think of this gift with hesitation. Even as we speak of Christmas joy and sing of "Joy to the World," sometimes there are lingering doubts about its reality. Mindful as we are of the widespread troubles in our world and the painful burdens that many bear in their individual lives, we tend to question the possibility of genuine joy in human experience. Joy seems to be a rare, almost whimsical commodity.

The motif of joy surrounds the Christ event. In his anticipation of the Messiah, Isaiah wrote, "You have multiplied the nation, you have increased its joy; they rejoice before you as with joy at the harvest, as people exult when dividing plunder" (9:3) At the birth of Jesus the angel proclaimed to the shepherds, "I am bringing you good news of great joy for all the people" (Luke 2:10). When it appeared that all hope of lasting joy had been dashed at Golgotha, Jesus' followers found an empty tomb and were seized "with fear and great joy" (Matt 28:8). As the wonder of the Christ event began to take hold on the early Christians, Peter could write, "Though you do not see him now, you believe in him and rejoice with an indescribable and glorious joy" (1 Pet 1:8).

The sensation of joy pervaded the life of the young Christian church and emerged as a dominant theme in the writings that became the New Testament. In the New Testament the word for "joy" occurs sixty times. The verb form, which means "to rejoice," is used seventy-two times. We do not fully understand the message of the New Testament until we see it as a book of joy.

Joy, however, is hardly a prevalent attitude among modern Christians. We seldom associate "enjoyment" with our religious expression. A better description of our approach might be "solemnity." Perhaps American religion is still shaded by the strong influence of our Puritan forebears who were deeply suspicious of anything which resembled pleasure. Piety, therefore, became equated with gloom, an idea that we have not been able to wipe completely from our thinking. Or, perhaps we have confused joy with a superficial kind of happiness and have been trapped into believing that joy does not exist until we have eliminated all our worries and attained all our desires.

Just what is the joy announced by angels and celebrated as God's gift to humanity? We begin to understand joy by acknowledging that it is a gift. We do not earn it by diligent effort nor discover it by careful searching. In fact, if joy becomes the object of a search, it will almost certainly not be found. Joy grows out of a healthy relationship with Jesus Christ and comes as one focuses on knowing and serving Christ, not on being joyful. Joy is a byproduct; it accompanies the relationship.

In his spiritual autobiography, C. S. Lewis tells about his quest for joy. He found himself at times trying substitutes for joy and at other times changing his definition of joy. It finally dawned on him that in order to know joy, one's whole attention and desire must be fixed on something else. So it happened one day that while riding in the sidecar of his brother's motorcycle on the way to the zoo, he found himself believing in Jesus Christ, a step he thought he could never take. As he recounted, he was "surprised by joy." At the end he wrote

> But what, in conclusion, of Joy? For that, after all, is what the story has mainly been about. To tell you the truth, the subject has lost nearly all interest for me since I became a Christian.[4]

This is the testimony of every joyful Christian. Joy is not a technique; there is no "how to do it" plan. Joy simply overtakes us in our experience with Christ.

We must learn our lesson on joy from Christ. I find it meaningful and helpful that Jesus' most pointed statements about joy were made on the eve of his death. In the upper room with his disciples he said, "I have said these things to you so that my joy may be in you, and that your joy may be complete" (John 15:11). A little later he said, "So you have pain now; but I will see you again, and your hearts will rejoice, and no one will take your joy from you" (16:22).

What kind of man, about to be executed like a criminal, could talk of joy and gladness? Either Jesus was beside himself or he knew resources of joy that could not be shaken. Sometimes, I feel, we need to humanize Jesus. Since Christmas is the celebration of the Incarnation, this might be a good time for that effort. What kind of a man was he? What do you think he was like? We call him a "man of sorrows and acquainted with grief" (Isa 53:3, RSV), and we are influenced by artistic portrayals that picture him as a man with a solemn face and a look of sadness in his eyes, a man either mild or serious. As Elton Trueblood points out in a little book called *The Humor of Christ,* maybe we have misrepresented him. The Christ we encounter in the Gospels has many contrasting features. "He is a Man of Sorrows, but He is also a Man of Joys."[5]

Look at the record. Little children clustered about him; he must have smiled easily and often. He associated with publicans and sinners. Had he been stern and judgmental, these social outcasts would have avoided him. He was asked why his disciples did not fast like those of John, and he replied, "The wedding guests cannot mourn as long as the bridegroom is with them" (Matt 9:15). I like to think that Jesus' personality was magnetic and that his company was a thing to be sought after and enjoyed. I also like to think that with his uninterrupted communion with the Father and his unselfish sharing with others, Jesus must have been the happiest of people. Freely he gave himself and his joy. He promised his own joy to his disciples and all who believe in him.

The source of our joy gives insight into what joy really is. It is a by-product of a life in God. Throughout the Bible, joy and gladness are consistently related to the whole life of God's people. Joy is not an isolated or occasional phenomenon. It is one of the constants in the Christian life. It is not destroyed by adverse circumstances; it does not wait for favorable events. It is a present reality.

Joy is a reality, because it is connected with the ways of God. This joy is not reached by living on the surface, however. It comes as one breaks through the surface and deals with the deep questions of his being. In the upper room Jesus was speaking from the depths. He knew the fate that awaited him. Of course, he felt dread. He struggled deep within, but he also knew joy. Looking back, the writer of Hebrews could say that Jesus "who for the sake of the joy that was set before him endured the cross" (12:2). The pattern is the same for anyone who will find lasting joy. There is the struggle of commitment and the pain of surrender, but out of the depths of such an experience emerges the joy, the joy of life eternal.

Jesus made two promises about his joy. It cannot be taken away. To be sure, we do not always feel the radiance that we would like. Events and situations will cloud our joy, and we should not be hypocritical and think that we have to wear a fixed smile to prove that we are religious. The same sensitivity that opens us to joy also exposes us to sorrow.

In *The Prophet,* Kahlil Gibran said it eloquently. When a woman asked of joy and sorrow, the prophet answered:

> Your joy is your sorrow unmasked. And the selfsame well from which your laughter rises was oftentime filled with your tears. And how else can it be? The deeper that sorrow carves into your being, the more joy you can contain. Is not the cup that holds your wine the very cup that was burned in the potter's oven? And is not the lute that soothes your spirit, the very wood that was hollowed with knives? When you are joyous, look deep into your heart and you shall find that it is only that which has given you sorrow that is giving you joy.[6]

No, joy does not mean that we will be unmoved by tragedy, that we will never shed a tear, that we will never fall into the slough of despondency. The person who cannot feel sorrow will never rise to the heights of enthusiasm or feel the surge of intense gladness. The occurrence of sorrow does not displace the joy of Christ, however, for we are repeatedly brought back to a confidence in God's presence and work in our lives.

Jesus also promised that our joy will be complete. It will go beyond any other kind of happiness. Like the bread of life that satisfies our spiritual hunger and the living water that quenches our spiritual thirst, the joy of Jesus Christ gives an all sufficient happiness that makes life supremely worth living.

In a sermon on the joy of Christ, Leonard Griffith cited this quote: "I have had more fun than any other man in the world. I have never met anyone who has had such fun as I have had." He asked who could have made such an extravagant statement? A libertine who had enjoyed his pleasures without regret? A world traveler? An adventurer? Then he said,

Those words were spoken by Dr. Frank Laubach, whose whole life has been one of sacrifice, a life dedicated to missionary service and especially to the cultivation of literacy among backward peoples. Explaining his "Each One Teach One" method, so successfully experimented with in Africa, Laubach declared in a jubilant voice, "You cannot describe the delight of people when they first discover they can read. Men go hysterical and women weep. No other work in the world could possibly have brought me greater happiness."[7]

Joy that is full and complete! What would we give for that precious treasure? Perhaps our search for joy and our frantic efforts to buy joy prevent our knowing it. Jesus did not tell us how to be joyful. Joy is a gift. He only said, "Abide in me as I abide in you. . . . I have said these things to you so that my joy may be in you, and that your joy may be complete" (John 15:10-11).

Day Six
The Gifts of Christmas: Peace

*Come to me, all you that are weary and are carrying heavy burdens, and I
will give you rest.*

—(Matt 11:28)

There is little secret as to why this winsome statement of
Jesus reaches into our hearts with such special appeal or
why it conveys such widespread hope. Every one of us lives
under the weight and pressure of personal burdens. Life demands
that we carry heavy loads and face hard work.

Some of our burdens are forced upon us by the unique circumstances of our lives; others we voluntarily assume. Some
burdens we would best be rid of, such as those that are brought on
by selfishness and guilt; others we do not want to surrender, such
as those that come as a result of love and commitment. Burden-
bearing is our common lot; we differ only with the type and
intensity of the burdens we carry. Most of the time we are so preoccupied with our own burdens that we forget that others are
hurting. Only as we truly come to know each other and get
beneath surface contact do we discover the tension and anxiety in
lives around us.

Some persons bear the heavy weight of loss and pain, burdens
that are inevitable in human experience, burdens over which we
seem to have no control. We know in our hearts that such burdens
must be accepted, but acceptance does not come easily. Why
death and suffering strike as they do we cannot fully understand.
Why conflict in family life and among friends is so common we
cannot fully explain. When we are touched by severe pain and
loss, we can only exclaim with the writer of Lamentations, "Look
and see if there is any sorrow like my sorrow, which was brought
upon me" (1:12).

Some persons bear the heavy weight of difficulty. Life never
seems smooth and tranquil. They never seem able to put things

together. For them God might be in heaven, but all's not right with their world! Their life is a grind and a drudgery.

Burdens are not always imposed on us from without, however. Some persons bear the weight of internal burdens. I think of the burden of disillusionment, the loss of confidence in goals, values, and other persons. To become disillusioned, to feel betrayed by those one has trusted, to believe that nothing can be done about a particular situation, finally to arrive at the point of self-pity is to experience an inward, spiritual decay and to carry a seemingly insurmountable burden.

I think of the burden of excessive personal expectations, the high aims we set for ourselves that go far beyond our reach. To compare our achievements with our aspirations can often leave us in the grip of frustration and failure. John Quincy Adams, the sixth President of the United States, was born into highly favorable circumstances. He was influenced by brilliant and gifted parents and educated in the best available schools. He had served as U.S. senator, Harvard professor, and American ambassador to major European countries by the time he was forty-five. At that point in his life, however, he wrote in his diary: "Two-thirds of my life have passed, and I have done nothing to distinguish it by unselfishness to my country and to mankind." Much later, at age seventy, after outstanding service as secretary of state, president, and member of Congress, he wrote: "My whole life has been a succession of disappointments. I can scarcely recollect a single instance of success in anything I ever undertook." History contradicts this evaluation, but John Quincy Adams was never able to make peace within himself. Throughout his life he carried the burden of frustration.

Many of our internal burdens we try to conceal from others out of fear of belittlement or rejection. But the burdens are real. No matter what our personal burden might be, we all ask the same questions: Does anyone understand? Does anyone care? Can anyone help? Can we find peace? We are like Dante who knocked at the gates of the Franciscan monastery at Lunigiana. When the friar opened the door and asked, "What do you wish?" Dante answered in a single word, "Peace."

This is precisely the promise of Jesus: "Come to me, all whose work is hard, whose load is heavy; and I will give you relief" (NEB). These words were first addressed to common people who were weary in their search for God and God's peace. His hearers had made their quest through organized religion, but the religion of the day had informed them that in order to find the peace of God, they must first be good. To their already overburdened lives, organized religion merely gave them the additional weight of rules and regulations. Follow these guidelines; make these sacrifices; attend these feasts and ceremonies; then you can have peace with God and peace with yourself!

Jesus introduced a different approach. Jesus taught that the knowledge of God and the peace of God do not come as the result of human achievement. Persons who said that only the "wise and understanding" could be pious or that only those who carefully observed the proper rituals and ceremonies would be acceptable to God were wrong. God's peace, Jesus said, is a gift to "infants," or those who are humble and receptive (Matt 11:25).

Study the way Jesus appealed to persons in the Gospels. He never put anyone down or added to their burdens. He never told people they were sinners or that they were going to hell. The only persons with whom he ever became angry were the religious leaders, and look at the persons with whom he freely associated: tax collectors and harlots, life's losers. He did not lecture them about their past. He simply asked that they come to him, believe in God's love, and accept God's hopes and plans for their lives. Oh, there was change. Change is necessary when you get close to Christ. The only requirement Jesus made was trust and a willingness to follow him.

"Take my yoke upon you," he said, "and learn from me." On the surface this might sound as though we are asked to exchange one burden for another, and in a sense this is true. To take upon ourselves the yoke of Christ means to enter into submission to him, to move from self-dependence to Christ-dependence. That's the rub, if you want to call it that, and it is never easy. We cannot put aside the truth that to know the peace of Christ we have to surrender ourselves to him, to give him our all.

In his spiritual autobiography C. S. Lewis describes his arrival at that realization. He wrote,

> Without words and (I think) almost without images, a fact about myself was somehow presented to me. I became aware that I was holding something at bay, or shutting something out. Or, if you like, that I was wearing some stiff clothing, like corsets, or even a suit of armor. I felt myself being given a free choice. I could open the door or keep it shut; I could unbuckle the armor or keep it on . . . I chose to open, to unbuckle, to loosen the rein.[8]

I think every one of us can agree with C. S. Lewis. Surrendering to Christ is not a once-for-all kind of decision. It's a choice repeated again and again whenever we return to the old defenses and revert to our own means of trying to cope with our sins and problems. Jesus invites us: "Come to me." He challenges us: "Take my yoke upon you."

"My yoke," Jesus says, "is good to bear," or "well-fitting." Jesus' listeners knew exactly what he meant. In that day, ox yokes were made of wood. An ox was measured by a carpenter, and a yoke was roughed out according to the measurements. When fitted to the ox, the yoke was further carved to prevent chafing on the neck of the beast.

There is another, and far more important, reason why the yoke of Christ fits so well. A yoke is made for two, never for one alone. Jesus does not impose upon his disciples a yoke that he himself does not also share. Therefore, in accepting his yoke, we allow him to enter our struggles with us, and he bears more than his share of the load. The idea that the coming of Christ means that God has taken up abode with us also means that God has taken upon God's self the load we carry.

Jesus took for granted that life will have burdens and that every life will be subject to some kind of yoke. Life cannot be completely carefree, and it cannot be aimless. We need commitments, responsibilities, and burdens—provided they are the right kind. So, we do not say that in Christ every problem is solved and every burden removed. That would be a total misrepresentation of the Christian faith. In Christ, though, we find "relief," "rest," or perhaps better still, "refreshment" so that we can handle our burdens victoriously.

We find what some call a "deep peace" settling over our thoughts, a peace that comes in knowing there is sufficient grace for our experience. This peace is not an escape from our burdens, our work, or other demands. Nor is it a Stoic fortitude in the face of difficulty. Rather, it is a kind of constant re-creation. It is a peace that comes in knowing we do not bear our burdens alone, that someone cares, understands, and helps.

Jesus did not attempt to avoid his burdens. In fact, he voluntarily took burdens on himself—our burdens and our sins—and he willingly shares himself with us when we come to him and accept his yoke. With this sharing of himself we discover not only a presence but also the peace we so deeply crave. This is the peace of Christmas.

Day Seven
The Gifts of Christmas: Hope

For in hope we were saved. Now hope that is seen is not hope. For who hopes for what is seen?

—(Rom 8:24)

In the eighth chapter of Romans Paul makes a surprising statement, "In hope we were saved," or as the King James renders it, "We are saved by hope." We would not dispute the place of hope in life, for life has no meaning without hope. The old saying, "While there is life there is hope," carries much greater force when it is reversed to say, "While there is hope there is life." Hope is the quality that fills life with expectancy and delivers it from despair.

We live in three dimensions. Each of us, at any given moment, lives in the past, the present, and the future. No matter how effectively we have dealt with the mistakes and burdens of the past, and no matter how effectively we have managed to work out a sense of well-being for the present, our lives are at best drab and incomplete unless they derive the strength of a hope for the future. We need a hope that can protect us from cynicism and discouragement.

What is meant by a hope that saves? Unfortunately, too often we think of hope as a vague desire for betterment, a desire that is based on luck or even chance. We have learned from experience that hope can be deceptive. Our ambitions go unrealized and our dreams unfulfilled. How can we say that we are saved by hope? How can we put our trust in something that might turn out to be empty? After all, we must come to grips with reality and face hard facts with clear vision. What did Paul mean when he said we are saved by hope?

Many times hope has been associated with progress. We cannot begin to understand Christian hope until we separate it from a false optimism about human progress. The philosophy of progress conceives of life as an upward movement from a lower to a higher level. It rests on the conviction that we can move toward perfection through reason and ability. The argument goes this way. As humans become more and more rational and expand their understanding of themselves and their world, they progress inevitably toward a better life.

There is much to be said for the philosophy of progress. Belief in human capabilities and the application of human understanding has brought about achievements that stagger the imagination. Looking back over just the immediate past, we can cite developments in science and technology that once we would never have thought possible. In terms of our living standards we have been able to witness immense progress.

But what about humanity? Is life qualitatively better for all material advancement? Are humans better prepared to live in harmony and justice with others on this planet where God has created one human family? Does progress bring hope? We all know the answers to these questions. Wars and tensions and shortages and greed have taught us that humans have used their powers as much for destruction as they have for good.

We need to recognize that scientific and material progress, for all their benefits, form no basis for hope. As enamored as we are with the notion of progress and human perfectibility, we must confess that it is not a Christian idea. As many leading thinkers point out, the philosophy of progress is a distortion of Christian hope. It is not a hope that saves.

We detect a glimmer of saving hope in the Old Testament prophets. The genius of the prophets was that they based their faith on historical fact. They recognized that God had revealed God's self to people in the events of their history, and they were aware of a dependence on God for a more complete self-unveiling as the only basis for hope. They began to anticipate a messianic kingdom of God's in-breaking.

Thus, we find Isaiah saying,

> In the wilderness prepare the way of the LORD, make straight in the desert a highway for our God. Every valley shall be lifted up, and every mountain and hill be made low; the uneven ground shall become level, and the rough places a plain. Then glory of the LORD

shall be revealed, and all people shall see it together, for the mouth of the LORD has spoken. (40:3-5)

As time passed, and as this hope took root, people would say, "I know that Messiah is coming . . . he will proclaim all things to us" (John 4:25).

When the time had fully come, the hope was realized. Yet, there is tragedy in the story. Only a few perceptive individuals recognized the Christ as the expression of their hope. The prophetic hope had been distorted, and the people of Israel generally had changed their hope in God into a nationalistic goal. Like persons today who see hope as material improvement, they longed for a messiah who would restore the nation. They were unprepared for the expression of love and righteousness that was embodied in the child of Bethlehem.

So we see the hope of the world, not enthroned in human hearts, but nailed to a cross, crucified as a rebel. And the hope appears, not to be victory, but defeat. For that reason we find the Christian understanding of hope emerging only after the Resurrection. The full truth about hope dawned on Jesus' followers only as they reflected on what God had done and would do. The New Testament writers began to speak of "Christ in you, the hope of glory" (Col 1:27). They saw the resurrection as the only basis for hope. As Peter wrote,

> Blessed be the God and Father of our Lord Jesus Christ! By his great mercy he has given us a new birth into a living hope through the resurrection of Jesus Christ from the dead (1 Pet 1:3).

New Testament hope has nothing to do with this-worldly prospects. It does not foresee an earthly utopia, not encourage materialistic optimism. It looks to the future and awaits the full manifestation of God's way in the return of our Lord. Therefore, Peter added, "Set all your hope on the grace that Jesus Christ brings you when he is revealed" (1:13). When we speak of Christ as the "hope of the world," we refer to his ultimate, direct, and manifest victory, the fulfillment of God's world purpose that is announced in the cross of Jesus Christ. This is the Christian hope; this is hope that saves!

Perhaps you are asking, as I am asking, what bearing this hope has on the here and now. Is it only a hope for the future that does not relate to the present? That is hardly the case. The kingdom of God, the ultimate fulfillment of which we anticipate, is now. It is present in Jesus Christ, and we participate in it insofar as we make his faith and work our own. The hope that saves is a gift that is ours to experience now. May our celebration of Christmas renew that hope within us. Consider three simple observations about it.

First, this hope that saves enlarges our vision to see the purposes of God at work in the world. While we observe a world that at times appears to be in shambles, and while we fret over the erosion of values, we affirm a faith in a God of morality who cares about righteousness and whose purposes will not be defeated. If this is our commitment, we can base our lives on something that is everlastingly true and solid. Trust does not come to hopelessness.

Consequently, we are delivered from the somber gloom that enfolds the mind when we are left only with human factors and human possibilities. We can look beyond what humans can do, and in our own lives, we can look beyond our own limitations and find a hope that nothing can shake. Therefore, hope is the "inseparable companion" of faith. As John Calvin, the great theologian of the Reformation, said:

> Hope is nothing else than the expectation of those things which faith has believed to have been truly promised by God. Thus, faith believes God to be true, hope awaits the time when truth will be manifested; faith believes that he is our Father, hope anticipates that he will show himself to be a Father toward us; faith believes that eternal life has been given to us, hope anticipates that it will sometime be revealed; faith is the foundation on which hope rests, hope nourishes and sustains faith.[9]

Can you see how this hope differs from a desire based on chance? Christian hope rests on what God has done. God has expressed hope toward us in Christ, an attitude of unconditional love, and the Christ of Christmas is a symbol that God is at work among us.

Second, the hope that saves, although it is future, gives meaning to this present life. The very fact that in Christ we find eternal life gives a worthwhileness to this life. Persons are never prepared for living in the present until they are prepared for living in the future. As Paul said, "If for this life only we have hoped in Christ, we are of all people most to be pitied" (1 Cor 15:19).

Christians are often accused of an unbalanced preoccupation with heaven and neglect of the problems of suffering and injustice. Certainly we cannot live for "pie in the sky by and by," but anyone who is honest will point out that the only hope that can build a better world is one that believes in a life beyond this world. The point is: only a trust that transcends everything earthly can enable us to live meaningfully and do our best work here and now.

Third, the hope that saves is a gift of God's grace. We have not invented it, and we cannot make it a part of our lives merely because we want to be hopeful. I like the approach of positive thinking. There is ample cause for optimism in this life. I feel that there is good in persons, and I have what sometimes borders on a naive trust in their motives and intentions. This outlook is grounded in the belief that life is good and hopeful because it has been touched by God, divinely created and redeemed. Because of God's work, I see every person's life as having amazing potential, and I am filled with hope.

If your hopes have been shattered, if your outlook has become overcast, if your spirit has become gloomy, I invite you this Christmastime to make another pilgrimage to the manger in Bethlehem. Along with the gifts of love, joy, and peace, there rests for you the gift of hope.

Notes

[1]Leo Buscaglia, *Bus 9 to Paradise* (Thorofare NJ: Slack, Inc., 1986) 131–32.

[2]Christina Rossetti, "In the Bleak Midwinter," *Scribner's Monthly* (Jan 1872).

[3]Paul Tournier, *The Meaning of Gifts* (Atlanta: John Knox Press, 1974) 34–35.

[4]C. S. Lewis, *Surprised by Joy* (New York: Harcourt, Brace & World, Inc., 1955) 238.

[5]Elton Trueblood, *The Humor of Christ* (New York: Harper & Row, Publishers, 1964) 20.

[6]Kahlil Gibran, *The Prophet* (New York: Alfred A. Knopf, 1956) 29.

[7]Cited by Leonard Griffith, *The Eternal Legacy* (New York: Harper & Row, Publishers, 1963) 135.

[8]C. S. Lewis, *Surprised by Joy* (New York: Harcourt, Brace & World, Inc., 1955) 224.

[9]John Calvin, *Institutes of the Christian Religion*, II, II, 42 (Philadelphia: The Westminster Press, 1960) 590.

The Fourth
Week of Advent

DRAMATIS PERSONAE

Day One
Angels, God's Messengers

In the sixth month the angel Gabriel was sent by God to a town in Galilee called Nazareth.

—(Luke 1:26)

What comes to your mind when you hear the word "angel"? Probably very little. We do not discuss angels very often in our daily conversations. I do not know anyone who has ever seen an angel. Angelology, an important study in medieval times, is not in the curriculum of our colleges today (or even our seminaries, for that matter). Angels are those shadowy figures in the background of some of the biblical stories. What place do they have in the modern world?

Yet, at Christmas, representations of angels are seen everywhere—on trees, on cards, in Christmas pageants, in outdoor displays. Even when they are all around us, we tend not to give angels serious attention. They are appendages to the Christmas story, not an integral part of it.

I acknowledge that in my personal Bible study I have never spent time thinking about angels. My most vivid concept of angels is that of the angel described by Thomas Wolfe, the cherished angel looking over the father's stonecutting shop in *Look Homeward, Angel*. At Christmas, as I study the birth narratives, I realize that perhaps I am missing something. Maybe we are neglecting something very significant.

The Bible contains hundreds of references to angels. It is fitting that the biblical student not notice them, because they never call attention to themselves. The Hebrew word for angel is *malak,* which means "messenger" or "ambassador." Angels in the Old Testament did not have the winged, ethereal connotation of later biblical literature. They usually appeared in the form of ordinary persons. Thus, the biblical writers spoke of "entertaining angels unawares" (Heb 13:2).

The Greek term *angelos,* from which our English word comes, means "a messenger from God" or a "spiritual being." Angels were present at crucial times in the life and ministry of Jesus. They heralded his birth, ministered to him after his temptation, strengthened him in Gethsemane, and announced his resurrection.

Paul de-emphasized angels. He wanted no kind of being between God and man. Paul's approach, I suppose, plus the gradual movement away from the metaphysical, turned the church away from any strong thought about angels.

Then we bring out the angels at Christmas! Let's move beyond our scientific certainties and intellectual closed-mindedness and think about angels. Angels are prominent in the Christmas stories. Four appearances are given. Gabriel, one of two angels mentioned by name in the New Testament, appeared to Zechariah, the father of John the Baptist. Gabriel also came to the maiden Mary at the well in Nazareth. An unnamed angel appeared to Joseph in a dream to tell him of the coming Savior. At the birth of Jesus, first one angel announced his arrival to shepherds, and then a chorus of angels sang his praises.

If you place the details of these stories in columns and look at them together, you find some remarkable similarities, a kind of key to a riddle. It might not convince you that angels are at work in your experience, but you might be more strongly attracted to the mysterious that, for all our knowledge, still surrounds almost every part of our lives.

These angelic appearances came while the human participants were going about their ordinary round of activities. The experiences were not contrived. Zechariah was a priest; he was in the temple burning incense before the altar of God. Mary was a young girl engaged to a poor carpenter; she was at the well drawing water, a daily chore for the women of Palestine. Joseph was the carpenter and fiance of Mary; he was sleeping fitfully, distraught over Mary's news that she was pregnant. The shepherds were tending their sheep in the fields outside Bethlehem.

Not one of these persons was on a religious retreat or seeking a word from God when God's messenger came. God comes to humans in God's own time and way and with the divine message. The experience itself can be awe-inspiring. Read the four stories and you will find that the first words of the angel in each case were "Fear not" or "Do not be afraid."

The awareness of an angel makes a person know that God is somehow involved in an experience, and the sudden consciousness of God can be overpowering. Call it fear, awe, or dread; it makes no difference. The presence of the holy brings a different sense of perspective. How can a human being feel anything but awe before God? When was the last time you felt it? Is that your fault or God's? Do you recognize the angelic?

Many persons do not acknowledge the angelic. They are conditioned not to do so, or they refuse to let themselves believe. Again, note the parallels in the birth stories and see that in each account the announcement of the angel was just too fantastic for belief. Zechariah and Elizabeth were too old to have a child. Mary was unmarried. How could she have a child? The Savior of the world? Born in a stable? From our perspective, Zechariah, Mary, Joseph, and the shepherds were extremely gullible. We certainly would not fall for something so foolish, would we? Why, we haven't believed in fairy tales since childhood—but then, that was about the time that the world changed from a place of wonder and possibility to a harsh place of "reality."

But what is reality? Christmas raises that question. What is real? Is it a problem or pain or sin or hurt? Or, is it the hope of salvation in a child? What's real? In a novel by Rebecca West, Cousin Jack puts down his flute and exclaims, "What's the good of music if there's all this cancer in the world?" Codellia, shaken with sorrow, replies through her tears, "What's the harm in cancer, if there's all this music in the world?"

Angels in the nativity accounts not only brought fantastic, almost unbelievable news, but also an atmosphere of celebration. "You will have joy and gladness," Gabriel said to Zechariah. Mary was able to say, "My soul magnifies the Lord." Joseph exulted in Immanuel, God with us. The angels on the hillside sang, "Glory to God in the highest."

Could we not benefit from rejoicing also? Do we not need a new sense of celebration and some fantastic, almost unbelievable news, to pull us out of the materialistic, technological, and humdrum existence that we have so carefully created and nurtured? So many possibilities are there if we hear the angels!

In the movie *Field of Dreams,* a young farmer named Ray Kinsella is walking through his cornfield when he hears a voice. It comes as little more than a whisper, but the words are unmistakable: "If you build it, he will come." At first there are only questions: Whose is the voice? Build what? Who will come? And then the revelation: Build a baseball field, and Shoeless Joe Jackson, the great star of the Chicago White Sox, will come.

The realization becomes a conviction and the conviction an obsession. Ray bulldozes a section of his cornfield and constructs a baseball diamond. Then he waits. One evening out of the tall corn steps Joe Jackson. Later he is joined by other White Sox players and members of the old New York Giants. Every day the teams play, but they are visible only to the farmer and his family and a social activist named Terence Mann—people who have heard the voice and who believe. The words of the voice become almost an invitation to the viewer: "If you build it, he will come."

Some people say that angels do not exist and have never existed, that the accounts of angels in the Bible are mythical embellishments of the stories. They say angels have no place in our understanding of things. I confess that heretofore this has been my own attitude toward angels, but more and more I see the limitations, not of angels but of my own understanding.

God still sends messengers. They might not have wings (though perhaps they do and we just can't see them) or be spiritual beings, but the messengers come because the message comes.

Look for these messengers. They might come in joy or pain, in defeat or challenge. They might come in simple ordinariness, but thank God they come. They might tell us fantastic things or usher us into the presence of God. One thing is certain we shall never be the same. Zechariah, Joseph, Mary, the shepherds—not one of them was ever the same after listening to the voice of angels.

Day Two
Herod, the Troubled Monarch

In the time of King Herod, after Jesus was born in Bethlehem of Judea, wise men from the East came to Jerusalem, asking, "Where is the child who has been born king of the Jews? For we observed his star at its rising and have come to pay him homage."

—(Matt 2:1-3)

Where does God fit in? That's an important question. This question begs to be asked during this special time of year. You and I need to ask where God fits in a season that is increasingly secularized and commercialized. Where does God fit in our so-called "religious" customs and celebrations? Where does God fit in our lives and thoughts as we anticipate the observance of Christ's birth? The season of Advent places this question before us. It must be honestly faced and clearly answered.

Deriving an answer sends us to the sources. We re-read, as carefully as possible, the stories and we think again about those persons immediately involved in the drama. We discover that we can learn something from each of the characters, even from someone like Herod the Great.

Herod occupied the throne in Jerusalem when Jesus was born. Herod was an interesting historical figure, and would have been an excellent subject for a Shakespearean tragedy. He was a man of talent, ambition, ruthlessness, and insecurity—a man of contrasting moods and unpredictable decisions. Herod was half Jew and half Idumaean. He came to power through his collusion with the Roman conquerors of Palestine. At first the Romans named him governor, but in 40 B.C. he was allowed to call himself king.

Herod confronted the dilemma of all regional rulers supported by Rome. He wanted to maintain favor with the empire, so he violently suppressed every form of local resistance. At the same time he deeply desired to be popular with the Jewish people. He built the magnificent temple in Jerusalem, in hard economic times he lowered taxes, during a famine he actually gave part of his own store of gold to buy corn for a starving populace. An able and efficient administrator, in many respects he deserved his title of Herod the Great.

Yet, Herod never received the affection and admiration he desired. He became almost insanely suspicious. Potential rivals to his position were promptly eliminated. His advisors became "yes men" who tried to stay out of his way. The occupant of the throne when Jesus was born was a man of power but also a man of obsessive fear, ready to protect his interest at any cost. One can easily understand why Herod was "troubled" when the magi appeared in Jerusalem saying, "Where is the child who has been born king of the Jews?"

Herod was "troubled" because talk of another king presented a threat to his precarious position. Matthew adds that "all Jerusalem (was troubled) with him," probably indicating that the people of the city feared what this unpredictable despot might do. Never mind what the report of the magi might mean to the life and religion of the country! The Christ was an intrusion upon a closed system.

For me, Herod and his world, shaky at best, represent life organized without reference to a higher power or a higher wisdom. Herod had a closed mind. He was not in the least concerned about a possible revelation from God that would aim for justice and righteousness, and elevate the welfare of his people. Such a perspective would bring judgment on the existing system, a situation that Herod would not tolerate.

Does Herod's attitude not describe a prevalent attitude in our world? Many people of our day have no time or concern for the claims we make about Jesus Christ. Individuals and societies alike have their goals, and they pursue them relentlessly. Anything that questions those goals is perceived as a threat. The modern person does not want to be "troubled" by talk of loving enemies, giving the kingdom of God priority over earthly kingdoms and sacrificing self for the will of God.

The response today is largely one of indifference. Have Christmas and get it over with, and get on with the business at hand. When you get right down to it, the celebrated miser in Charles Dickens' *A Christmas Carol* had nothing against Christmas itself. His gripe essentially was that people were using the holiday as an excuse for cheating a man out of his hard-earned money, getting out of an honest day's work, or engaging in other forms of nonsense—all in the name of goodwill. Or, in Scrooge's words, the observance of Christmas was "no excuse to pick a man's pocket every twenty-fifth of December." Don't take it seriously, and no one is offended. Engage in a sincere search for the newborn king, and he becomes a threat—and threats must be taken seriously!

Herod was not indifferent; he was a man of action. He knew how to handle threats. His policy was to destroy them. Herod was no novice in the art of murder. He had killed his friend, Hyrcanus II, who had once saved his life. He had ordered the death of his wife, Mariamne, and three of his sons, Antipater, Alexander, and Aristobulus. Herod's atrocious acts had prompted the Emperor Augustus to say that it was much safer to be Herod's pig than Herod's son.

Summoning the chief priests and scribes from their study cells, Herod inquired about the ancient prophecies concerning the messiah. He would be born in Bethlehem of Judea, Herod was told. Then to the Eastern wise men, Herod said, "Go and search diligently for the child; and when you have found him, bring me word so that I may also go and pay him homage."

I imagine that Herod consulted the Jewish religious leaders with disgust. He cared nothing for their scriptures. He was content with his own Greco-Roman gods who made no demands on his thought and action. Yet, he was willing to use any tool at his disposal for his own purposes, and his lie to the magi was nothing more than one more political ploy.

Suspicion and deceit proved to be Herod's downfall. Interestingly, Herod the Great, a man otherwise so meticulous to detail, sent the magi to Bethlehem alone. Why did he not send a squad of soldiers to carry out his true wishes, the murder of the child? Perhaps he wanted to destroy the baby himself. Herod's inability to trust even his own army frustrated his plans. The magi did not return.

In the next scene, we see the horrendous cruelty of a desperate man. Realizing that he had been tricked by the magi, Herod flew into a furious rage. He ordered the massacre of all male children in Bethlehem under two years of age. Matthew's gospel is the only record of this horrible act, and some scholars have questioned the accuracy of this report. Bethlehem was not a large village, so the number of children slain was probably twenty or thirty. A tyrant could sweep this kind of thing under the rug. After all, there was no avenue whereby people could complain about the actions of the king.

Consider the meaning of this deed! Evil can perpetuate itself only by greater evil. Herod had his opportunity. The Christ child did not really pose an immediate threat to Herod. The messiah was to be a blessing, not a curse, but he did not "fit into" Herod's scheme. To counter him, Herod resorted more and more to the violence by which he had always lived.

The slaughter of the innocents was one of Herod's last acts. Painfully and hopelessly ill, an old man without family and friends, Herod faced the end of life in disillusionment. He had never received the adulation he had wanted. At least, he decided, there should be mourning at his death. So Herod imprisoned the leading Jewish citizens in an arena in Jericho with the command that they be put to death when he himself died. When news of Herod's demise arrived, however, the prisoners were set free, and the death of the tyrant was welcomed as a relief instead of a time of national mourning.

Herod's story is a classic example of a person who had no place in his life for the Christ child. Nothing in his background prepared him to understand what God was doing. For him the Christ child was perhaps just one more problem to be solved. Rulers of his day survived only by intrigue and assassination.

Maybe Herod's story serves as a warning against living in a closed system. At many points in life, new truth can break in upon us; we must be open to receive it. The celebration of the Christmas season each year provides us with opportunities for a fresh appreciation of the beauty and a deeper understanding of what God has done in Jesus Christ. We should not regard these opportunities as a threat but as a possibility.

Herod's story also indicates that without the ability to receive new truth and allow it to judge us, we are left more and more to our own tired old devices. We push harder and harder to achieve our aims, pile evil upon evil, and end far worse than we were. Where does God fit in? This question must be before us. Where do we fit in? This is the question that the silent, innocent child of Bethlehem brings back to our world as we think of his coming.

Day Three
Joseph, a Righteous Man

Now the birth of Jesus the Messiah took place in this way. When his mother Mary had been engaged to Joseph, but before they lived together, she was found to be with child of the Holy Spirit. Her husband Joseph, being a righteous man and unwilling to expose her to public disgrace, planned to dismiss her quietly.

—(Matt 1:18-19)

The Christmas story is about the birth of a child. The arrival of a child transforms a couple into a family. The birth of the Christ child has transformed the whole human race into a family. In a sense, therefore, we are all part of the Christmas family. Let's think "Christmas family" as we rethink the stories of Joseph and Mary.

We often overlook Joseph when we survey the stable scene in Bethlehem. In our imagination he is there standing devotedly over the manger or welcoming the visitors to the stall, or seeing to Mary's needs. Yet, he seems almost a part of the background. Not a single word from Joseph is recorded in the birth stories in Matthew and Luke. Little is said about him. Matthew gives one note about his character: he was "a righteous man"—but that comment is heavy with meaning.

Who was this "righteous man" who became the father of the Christ child? Joseph was a Judean with a proud heritage. He was a descendant of King David. Bethlehem, the birthplace of David, was his ancestral home. Joseph's family, however, had no wealth or power. The young Joseph became a carpenter. Perhaps he found it difficult to earn a living in Bethlehem. At some point he moved north to the town of Nazareth. There he settled and built a house for himself and his future family. Probably Joseph's house was little more than a small structure over one of the many caves in Nazareth.

Once established in his trade, Joseph began to think about marriage. There were steps in the Jewish marriage procedure of those days. First was the engagement, a pairing usually made by the parents or a professional matchmaker. Sometimes a boy and girl were chosen for each other when they were very young. Marriage was a very serious matter; a number of people were involved in the selection process. Love between the young man and the young woman was not excluded, however. Either person upon coming of age could reject the chosen partner and break the engagement. If love developed, and both the young man and woman were willing, they entered the second stage: the betrothal. The betrothal was a binding contract, to be terminated only by divorce. It lasted for a year, during which the couple might be called husband and wife, but they did not live together. At the end of the year of betrothal, they were married.

Joseph was betrothed to a young girl by the name of Mary. Their preparation for marriage was temporarily interrupted. According to Luke, Mary left Nazareth to visit her cousin Elizabeth far to the south, near Jerusalem. Elizabeth was getting on in years, but to everyone's surprise she was expecting a baby.

Mary was gone for three months. When she came back, she told Joseph that she, too, was pregnant. If you can, let Mary and Joseph be real persons, not ceramic figures in a creche. Let them have the same emotions that you and I feel. Joseph knew that the child Mary was carrying was not his. Matthew is specific: Joseph and Mary had not been living together.

Joseph was shocked and hurt. Something had to be done. Even in the best of circumstances the anticipation of a baby demands that something be done. What were Joseph's options? He could divorce Mary and subject her to public humiliation. Legally, she could have been stoned for her obvious adultery. Or, Joseph could marry her and give her respectability and subject himself to shame. To marry her would make it appear that Joseph was guilty of adultery and that Mary was his victim.

At this point in the story, Matthew tells us about Joseph's integrity: "Joseph, being a righteous man." The word in Matthew's account is *dikaios,* which means "just" or "righteous." Well, what does a righteous man do in such a situation?

Most of the time a righteous person will choose to make a show of his/her righteousness. You can imagine the acclaim Joseph would have received had he followed the normal procedure for divorce, had he taken Mary into the street in Nazareth and there proclaimed three times, "I divorce you"—no wait, no hassle, no legal fees. His character would have been vindicated. Everyone would have remarked about Joseph's goodness and whispered about Mary's being an adulteress.

To be righteous, though, means to do what is right—which is not so easy. Joseph, the righteous man, took the difficult course. He avoided the extremes. Joseph decided that he would have to divorce Mary but that he would do so quietly, to spare her shame and danger. He apparently gave no thought to what his neighbors might say. He made his choice.

Then the angel came on divine visitation. God let Joseph in on what was happening. Isn't that the way it always occurs? You go through the agony of making a terrible decision, and then there is some kind of insight or bit of information that would have been very welcome earlier. Why doesn't God send the angel sooner? Why is our "righteousness" tested over and over?

Everything came into focus with the words of the angel:

> Joseph, son of David, do not be afraid to take Mary as your wife, for the child conceived in her is from the Holy Spirit. She will bear a son, and you are to name him Jesus, for he will save his people from their sins. (Matt 1:20-21)

Following this announcement we see another dimension of righteousness. Joseph was unquestioningly obedient to what he perceived to be divine leadership.

What about our response to the claims of the Christmas story? "Conceived of the Holy Spirit"—we still do not know what that means or how Jesus came to be. We use terms such as "the virgin birth" and make "conceived of the Holy Spirit" a part of our confession of faith, but we do not understand these mysteries. Are we righteous enough to act on something we don't understand if we think it is a directive from God?

Joseph was. In fact, Joseph was a man of action. Go through the birth narratives in Matthew and Luke and notice the verbs that follow Joseph's name: "Joseph resolved" . . . "considered" . . . "did as he was commanded" . . . "rose and departed" . . . "went and dwelt" . . . These are strong verbs; they depict Joseph as a man of decision, obedience, and action.

On the basis of the words of an angel that appeared to him in a dream, Joseph completely altered his life's plans, endured local gossip, spent at least two years away from his carpenter's shop, took Mary and the baby to Egypt (a difficult trip even today), and placed himself in grave danger. A righteous man will do that! And Joseph did all these things "quietly." Joseph is the only character in the birth stories (save the baby himself) from whom no word is recorded. Read the first two chapters of Matthew and Luke. We have speeches by angels, Elizabeth, Zechariah, and Mary; statements from the shepherds, the magi, and even Herod the Great; and songs and affirmations from Simeon and Anna, the prophetess. But not a word from Joseph! Not that he could not speak; he demonstrated his love through what he did.

Yet, Joseph's message is plain. His witness is there for us to see— and to imitate! Joseph carefully and lovingly brought Mary eighty miles south to Bethlehem in the late stages of her pregnancy. He found a place (a humble place, but a place) for the child to be born. He saw to it that the child was named and circumcised and presented in the great temple at the proper time. He protected Mary and the child from Herod's wrath. He made the child that was not his own his own.

Joseph provided Jesus with the security of a stable and righteous home life. We know from the story of Jesus in the temple at the age of twelve that each year Joseph interrupted his work for ten days to take his family to Jerusalem for Passover. He must have taken Jesus each sabbath to the synagogue, for one writer said that on the sabbath Jesus "went to the synagogue, as his custom was." Joseph must have been a devout Hebrew father in teaching his son the Scriptures, for Jesus knew them at age twelve, and when he began his ministry, he had a mastery of the scriptures that made people say that he taught with authority (Matt 7:29).

Hear the legacy of Joseph in the teachings of Jesus. At the conclusion to that marvelous body of ethical teaching we call the Sermon on the Mount, we hear Jesus the carpenter's son saying, "Everyone then who hears these words of mine and acts on them will be like a wise man who built his house on rock" (Matt 7:24). Was he remembering Joseph's patient instruction in building on a solid foundation? When Jesus called all the tired, lonely, and hurting people in the world to rest and said "Take my yoke upon you" (11:29), was he recalling all those times in the carpentry shop when his father would painstakingly fit the yokes he made onto the oxen that they would be a help instead of a burden?

The example, the faith, the dedication of the silent but righteous father speak even today in the words of the son. Joseph was a righteous man! God, give us righteous fathers. Let us who are fathers be righteous so that the Christmas family might be complete.

Day Four
Mary, the Handmaid
of the Lord

Then Mary said, "Here am I, the servant of the Lord; let it be with me according to your word." Then the angel departed from her.
—(Luke 1:38)

Christians tend to pay either too much or too little attention to Mary, the mother of Jesus. Some of them refer to her as Mary "the Mother of God." The deification of Mary began in the third and fourth centuries. Through the years some Christians have come to believe that Mary was born by Immaculate Conception, was a lifelong virgin, and ascended bodily into heaven. This kind of concentration on Mary, I would suggest, is a distortion. The New Testament contains no basis for such claims.

Yet, those who reject Marian theology often pay Mary too little attention. They speak of the miraculous birth of Jesus, but they overlook the fact that Christ's coming was through the process of physical birth and that that birth occurred because a young Hebrew girl went through a bewildering pregnancy and accepted all that pregnancy and birth require —the wonder, the morning sickness, the discomfort, the pain, and, in all likelihood, the postpartum depression. We piously say that as Jesus grew he "increased in wisdom and in stature, and in divine and human favor" (Luke 2:52). To the loving mother it was anything but automatic. Mary cared for Jesus through this growth. She watched him change from an adorable baby to an active toddler, from a precocious eight-year-old to an anxious adolescent, and finally to an intense young adult whom she could not understand. We should not deify Mary; neither should we take for granted her life and sacrifice. Her contributions to our faith are highly significant.

Mary was a young girl of Nazareth, probably fourteen to sixteen years of age when the angel Gabriel appeared to her. That was the normal age for betrothal, and Mary was betrothed to a young man named Joseph. In Hebrew her name was Miriam, which meant "bitter myrrh." This name had gloomy connotations. Maybe it was given to her because her family was poor; Mary herself said she was of "low estate." First-century Christian tradition says that Mary's parents were named Joachim and Anna and that they were members of priestly families. This would fit with the note in Luke that Mary was a cousin of Elizabeth, who also was in the priestly line.

Mary's name appears frequently in the Gospels. From these references we can detect some of her personal characteristics. Mary was introspective. She knew how to apply the scriptures to the message of the Christ child. She "pondered" what happened at Jesus' birth. She "marveled" at the words of Simeon. Mary was far from passive, however. Her assertiveness was evident. She sharply reprimanded Jesus when he lagged behind in the temple. She insisted that he do something at the wedding feast in Cana. She would not be deterred even before his cross. Although her son had been deserted by his followers, she was there. A pensive and forthright woman, Mary was, above all, a woman of trust. She trusted God; she believed the prophecies. Like most Hebrew girls, Mary might have prayed that she could be the one to bear the long-awaited messiah.

To this young woman the angel Gabriel appeared. Note the words of the story carefully. The angel said, "Greetings, favored one! The Lord is with you" (Luke 1:28). Mary was "perplexed" at what the angel said, not at the angelic visit. In that day belief in angels was common; nowhere in the New Testament is the appearance of an angel viewed as something extraordinary. But "favored one!" What grace! To be favored by God is a tremendous blessing, but consider what goes with God's favor. Through grace God not only blesses and sustains, but chooses and puts to divine use. In God's economy the time had come for the birth of the messiah, the anointed one. Mary would be the one through whom this gift to humankind would come.

"Favored one" should fill a person with awe, with dread and wonder. Think about Mary's story. If she had wanted unbroken family happiness, being God's favored one did not give it to her. It meant danger, uncertainty, and heartbreak. How many mothers have to watch the execution of their sons? If Mary had wanted ease and prosperity, being God's favored one did not bring those things. It meant moving from Nazareth to Bethlehem to Egypt to Nazareth, later to Jerusalem, and, finally, in her old age, to Ephesus to live under the care of John and the church.

Mary might tell you and me to beware of asking for God's favor. God's favor, the divine grace and blessing, is absolutely incomparable. Without it life is not life. God's favor means also a call to service, a summons to commitment and, very likely, to sacrifice. Little wonder that Mary the Jewish maiden was "perplexed" at the words of the angel!

"You will conceive in your womb and bear a son," Gabriel said, "and you shall call his name Jesus" (v. 31). Even Mary the trusting teenager had her questions: "How can this be, since I have no husband?" (v. 34)

This is one of two statements in the Gospels that call attention to Mary's virginity. On these brief comments we base the doctrine of the virgin birth. It might do us well to see why it was so important to the Gospel writers, Christian thought, and the Christian church.

Many today insist on the Virgin Birth as a means of explaining Jesus' divinity. It is unthinkable that Jesus would have been conceived in the usual way. Well, the early church didn't think that way. By the time the Gospels of Matthew and Luke were written, the Christian church was facing a heresy called Docetism. The Docetists held that Christ had been a divine being who only seemed to be human. Matthew and Luke were actually stressing the fact that Jesus had a "real live human mother," that he was human as well as divine.

Nor did the writers mention the virgin birth to show that Jesus' birth was miraculous. They believed that every birth was a miracle. One Jewish saying held that in the birth of every child there are three participants: the mother, the father, and the Spirit of God. The whole point of the Virgin Birth for then and now is that God has come in human form, that God has become man through a Jewish peasant girl.

If Mary had any more questions, they were resolved with Gabriel's affirmation: "For nothing will be impossible with God" (v. 37). Mary's wonder and questions melted into acquiescence: "Her am I, the servant of the Lord; let it be with me according to your word" (v. 38). This is a marvelous statement, a kind of life motto. If, as tradition says, Mary was a poor girl and possibly an orphan, if she was a servant girl or handmaid, to the more affluent families of Nazareth, her response to the angel was simply a transfer of servanthood from others to God. It was the gift of herself to the will of God. What a beautiful thought! What can one give God but oneself? That's just what God expects.

What a powerful witness to Jesus Christ! The giving of what one is! And how typical of a mother! Therefore, I said at the beginning that we should not distort Mary by making her divine or by ignoring her sacrifice and feelings. I think there are few better witnesses to the Christ than the person who gave him life and then had to watch as others took it. Few affirmations are more powerful than the simple declaration, "Here am I, the servant of the Lord." We can learn from the Christ child and his mother that we gain life by giving it. What better time than this season to discover this?

A missionary to Ecuador has identified with the poor, the dispossessed, and powerless people of that nation. Hunger, filth, sickness, and human suffering are the substance of his days. As he travels from one mission point to another, he might stop to help a man start his car, hug a dirty child who runs out to meet him, or give food to a hungry mother and her baby.

This missionary occasionally has visitors from the U.S. who spend a few days with him. One such guest became frustrated with his friends apparently wasted efforts. He asked, "Why are you burning yourself out in this small country when there is no hope for social reform? Isn't there something more important for you to do?" The missionary replied, "Every person's life is like one tiny grain of sand, and each of us must decide where to lay our grain on the beach of life. I have chosen to lay mine beside these suffering people."

From Bedlam to Bethlehem

Mary made her choice; she chose to be the "servant of the Lord," to give herself to God's leadership. The missionary in Ecuador and millions like him today and through the centuries have made their choices.

You and I must choose. There's no angel nor anything supernatural about us, but when we come to see the Christ child, it's as if a voice says to each of us, "Greetings, favored one!" We are all objects of God's grace. We are all chosen for great works. We ought to be troubled by such news, especially at Christmas.

Day Five
The Shepherds,
Society's Rejects

In that region there were shepherds living in the fields, keeping watch over their flock by night. Then an angel of the Lord stood before them, and the glory of the Lord shone around them, and they were terrified.

—(Luke 2:8-9)

John Carlson, a young Lutheran minister in Minnesota, gained national attention a few years ago with an innovative idea in his work with young people. He decided that there should be a special party on the night of the senior prom for those youth who did not have dates. He had observed that senior prom night was an occasion for hurt feelings and deep depression for many high schoolers. Not to have a date for the prom was to be declared a reject, a loser. What was even sadder, Carlson concluded, was that being dateless on prom night seemed to be the finishing blow to years of rejection and put-downs.

Whether by design or accident, the senior high prom seemed to be reserved for the beautiful and the popular. So John Carlson planned an alternative. He called it the Reject Prom. Everyone who did not have a date for the senior prom was given a special invitation. The Reject Prom was held on the same night as its counterpart. Carlson went to great lengths to make sure it was a blowout party.

Once this idea took hold, there was no stopping it. Every year the number of seniors attending the Reject Prom grew. It began to get press coverage. Timex Corporation gave watches to the youth who came. Other companies joined in and overwhelmed the participants with gifts and souvenirs. Before long kids who could get dates to the senior prom decided not to; they wanted to be at the special party for rejects.

One cannot help but think that our Lord would be delighted with such a party. After all, those to whom the announcement of the birth of Jesus was first made and who were the first to celebrate our Lord's coming were rejects. The shepherds are always there in our mental picture of the first Christmas. To us they bring a certain charm to the scene, which merely shows how far imagination removes the Christ event from reality.

At the time Jesus came, shepherds were not "charming" people. They were outcasts. Shepherds were generally considered to be dirty, dishonest, and nonreligious. They were despised by "good" people. They were tolerated because they performed a necessary task, but their vocation had no honor whatsoever. Shepherding was something one fell into when he failed at everything else. Shepherds were rejects, but they were the first to be invited to participate in God's new order.

That shepherds were first to come to the Christ is highly significant. Their calling came to symbolize Jesus' spirit and ministry. He identified with the rejects and failures of the world. Jesus was accused of being a "friend of tax collectors and sinners." He said, "I have come to call not the righteous but sinners to repentance" (Luke 5:32).

Later Jesus told a story about God's great party, the banquet of the kingdom. When the invited guests declined, the householder sent his servants out into the "streets and lanes of the town and bring in the poor, the crippled, the blind, and the lame" (14:21). In effect, this man was filling his house with society's rejects and failures. Jesus' message was unmistakable: God has not forgotten the forgotten of our world, nor rejected the rejected, nor lost faith in the failures. The shepherds should always remind us of this fact.

Look at their story. It is one of the most noble in the Gospels. The shepherds were at their work in the fields outside Bethlehem when the angel of the Lord appeared. The angel said,

> Be not afraid, for see, I am bringing you good news of great joy for all the people; to you is born this day in the city of David a Savior, who is Messiah, the Lord. (2:11)

We are impressed initially by the response of the shepherds. At the announcement the shepherds said, "Let us go now to Bethlehem and see this thing that has taken place" (2:15), and they went "with haste." The shepherds were simple men. They did not have to raise all the questions that others might have asked. When the magi came to Jerusalem asking about the birth of a new king, there was no excited response. Everyone was troubled. Then there was a search of the scriptures for verification. When angels come today (and they do come!), we ask about the power of coincidence or the state of our minds at a given time. The shepherds simply responded.

When they came to the baby, they rejoiced. Who knows what they thought or understood? They knew only that they were people of need and that they were in the presence of one who was theirs, one given by God to supply need. The word "savior" held incalculable appeal, for they were in need of a savior. Herein, is the key element in the story. The situation is not that God rejects the accepted and accepts the rejected or that God does not like people who are beautiful, popular, wealthy, or powerful. Not at all! The situation is that those who seem to have it all together either deny or refuse to face their need for a savior.

I will never forget an experience I had in my first church staff position following seminary. I put together a program on drug abuse and provided a meeting for parents. I secured an excellent counselor for the parents' meeting. His assignment was to help parents identify the signs of possible drug use by their teenagers and to get the problem into the open. I knew that several of our youth were involved with alcohol and marijuana. (This was the 1970s.) Not a single one of the parents of those youth was present. Later, one of them said to me, "I was afraid that if I came, people would think my son was using drugs."

In many ways we consciously deny or inadvertently fail to recognize our need. Junk bond king Michael Milken was fined $600,000,000 and sentenced to ten years in prison for illegally manipulating our financial system to arrange major corporate mergers in the 1980s. He was surprised with his jail term. In a letter to Judge Kimba Wood, Milken wrote, "I never dreamed that I could do anything that would result in being a felon." For years he had lived by the maxim, "Take no prisoners; brook no opposition." He had wanted to rule the financial world and would do anything to achieve his aims. Even at the end Milken was neither a failure nor a reject to himself or to his contemporaries. His "sin," according to many persons, was that he was not prudent; he got caught.

As long as we have the mind-set that there is no right or wrong, that we are really okay people who just need to be careful, that the idea of failure applies always to someone else, we will not hear the word "savior" nor respond to the announcement of his coming. There is certainly no cause for rejoicing! Who needs him? Herod did not need a savior; he was a man of power. Never mind that he was crazed with jealousy, fear, and suspicion; he had his authority. The religious leaders did not need a Savior; they had the law and were, by virtue of their position, people of honor. Why go traipsing off to search for a baby?

The shepherds were unencumbered by power, position, or sophistication. They were encumbered by a need for what the Christ child came to fill. Thus, they were able to respond quickly and completely, and they were able to rejoice simply in the presence of the Christ. Note also that the shepherds returned to their tasks. They did what God wants all Christians to do. They took the spirit of the Christ, the spirit God has revealed in our Lord, back with them. Of course, they were changed. There is no question but that they were completely transformed. They returned "glorifying and praising God for all they had heard and seen" (Luke 2:20). But they returned! They returned to their tasks. A person may miss the significance of God's revelation and call because there is always a return. We want a magical change in our surroundings. We think God should lift us out of difficult situations and make life easy or different.

Whether the circumstances change or not is beside the point. I find something touching in the shepherds at the manger scene, something deeply symbolic. God has come in Christ to call all of the failures, the rejects, and the misfits of this world to salvation. If you know that you belong to one of these categories, how blest you are! (Jesus later said that.) He's for you; you can respond in trust and rejoice without reservation. If you cannot see that or will not acknowledge that you are in need of help, you might miss the party—not because you were not invited, but because you did not recognize your own name on the invitation.

Day Six
The Magi, Men
of True Wisdom

In the time of king Herod, after Jesus was born in Bethlehem of Judea, . . .
they [wise men] set out; and there, ahead of them, went the star that they
had seen at its rising, until it stopped over the place where the child was.
When they saw that the star had stopped, they were overwhelmed with joy.
—(Matt 2:1-11)

Each of the major divisions of our Bible begins with an account of a search. Early in the pages of the Old Testament we see the Lord God coming into the Garden of Eden in search of Adam and Eve, saying, "Where are you?" The first pair had turned away from God. They had broken the perfect fellowship they shared with their maker through willful disobedience. Under the weight of their guilt and shame, Adam and Eve tried to hide from God, but God came seeking them. Here in the account of the wise men from the East we have the corresponding side of God's search for humanity—our search for God.

The visit of the magi enhances the beauty and the appeal of the Christmas story. But this account is not merely an embellishment; it is not included to give charm to the narrative. Matthew saw the coming of the magi as the approach of people "from east and west, and from north and south" (Luke 13:29) to the new king and his new kingdom. The magi represent a universal yearning for what God has done in Jesus Christ.

The mystery surrounding the wise men stimulates our curiosity. In the second chapter of Matthew's Gospel, these striking figures enter the story abruptly and then, just as quickly, go out again into obscurity. We do not know their names or their origin. We do not even know how many there were. Early tradition held that there were twelve wise men. We have come to think in terms of three, however, because there is mention of three gifts. Legend has given them names—Caspar, Melchior, and Balthasar—and efforts have been made to describe them—Caspar as a young man who found a young king, Balthasar as a man of middle age who discovered a Savior, Melchior as an elderly man who found in Christ a reliable companion. These ideas are based on legend; the wise men remain figures of mystery.

The best historical evidence we have comes from the Roman Herodotus who said that the magi were part of a Median tribe in the empire of the Persians. An attempt by the Medes to take power from the Persians failed. The magi gave up ambitions for political power and became a tribe of priests. They became in Persia what the Levites were in Israel. The magi studied philosophy, natural science, and religion. Many were holy men who sought the truth.

This attitude gave the magi their unique place in the Christmas story and a strong appeal for us. Herod's perspective was not adequate. The perspective of anyone who sees life only in terms of power and position omits a very basic part of life itself: the need for truth and meaning and fulfillment. Something within our make-up will not allow us to be content until the question of meaning is addressed. The wise men touch a responsive chord in our hearts; they symbolize a quest to which too little attention is given: the search for true fulfillment.

Our hurried lives and preoccupations with carrying out our roles or "just getting by" do not encourage a search for meaning. Some people will say that the here and now and the pleasure or gain we can get for ourselves is more important. The desire for meaning is sometimes even perceived as unhealthy.

Victor Frankyl points out, however, that one is neither sick nor abnormal when he/she questions life's meaning and value. This search, Frankyl says, "only proves that one is truly a human being."[1] It is the clearest distinction between a human being and an animal. To seek meaning is to act like a person is supposed to act!

The struggle for meaning is not a comfortable search. It requires that we get out of our mental and spiritual ruts. We can easily postpone the search, because we have many diversions to keep us occupied, but we cannot avoid it all together. All persons will sooner or later have those "crisis" moments of experience when they have to ask what they believe in and stand for, when they have to ask why they are here and where life is going. Whenever you stop to ask, "Why?" you raise what is at the bottom a religious question, and you set out on your search for meaning.

The need for meaning can prompt a person to do strange things. The idea persists that meaning lies somewhere else other than in one's normal routine. This notion leads a person to leave school, work, or family to "go off and find herself." Occasionally we read of a man who will sell everything he has, buy a boat, and sail around the world in search of something. Of what he is not quite sure, and where it is to be found he is not quite certain. We know the feelings that lie behind such a radical action and even feel a twinge of envy ourselves. Somewhere "out there," we think, meaning is to be found.

Note that the magi located their guide toward fulfillment while they were pursuing their normal activities. In ancient times people believed in astrology. They believed that the stars, in their unvarying courses, represented order in the universe and that, by understanding the fixture of the stars and constellations, they could foretell the future and learn about human destiny. Faithfully, as students of the heavens, the magi sought what the stars would tell them. We do not know what the brilliant star these men saw could have been. Whether it was a meteor, a planetary conjunction, or some miraculous light we can only guess. Yet, they saw something unique and knew that they must follow its movement.

God speaks to persons within the ordinary, but when attention is captured, when we perceive that God has something extraordinary for us to hear, we must act with abandon. The magi gathered provisions for a journey and set out. Over hundreds of miles of treacherous terrain they traveled, always with their vision fixed on the star. Through weary days and nights they tracked the star across a featureless desert, sustained by hope and excitement.

The guidance God provided the magi is indicative of divine guidance for anyone who makes a sincere search for God. In the darkness of sorrow or the depth of troubles, there is sufficient grace and encouragement to look further, think deeper, and feel with more sensitivity. Our problem is that we do not persevere. We quit too soon. We are too ready to give up the quest and return to our old ways.

Several years ago a plane flying over the Swiss Alps developed engine trouble. Many Americans were on board, including Bob Hope. The pilot began looking for a place to land. As would be expected in such an emergency, the passengers became quiet and began to pray. After a short while, the pilot located a runway, and the plane came in for a safe landing. Bob Hope stood up in the silence and said, "Now, folks, you can go back to the same old life you gave up twenty minutes ago."

We really cannot go back to the same old life and ways of thinking once we have begun the search, once we have come to what Paul Tillich called "the frontier of being." We can never again be content with things as they are. We have sensed that life has greater possibilities. The old way is no longer so comfortable. We must move forward.

The journey of the magi led them to Jerusalem and then to Bethlehem. At long last the star stopped, and beneath its radiance they found the object of their search: the newborn king. Going into the house where the young family was staying, the magi bowed before the child and worshiped.

Words are unnecessary, perhaps even impossible, when we discover the relationship that gives life meaning. There was no explanation about the child, for explanations are not necessary when we come to feel for certain that we have found that which makes life worthwhile. Reasons can neither prove nor disprove faith. There was only reverence. And that is necessary! John Ruskin once made this comment about the magi:

> These men, for their own part, came—I beg you very earnestly to note this—not to see, nor talk—but to do reverence. They were neither curious nor talkative, but submissive.[2]

In addition to reverence, the magi brought gifts that they adoringly presented to the child. We must also bring gifts, the greatest of which is ourselves.

Wise men and women, wise young people, wise boys and girls still seek the Christ. They face with open eyes that haunting need deep within for fulfillment and meaning. They look for the star that shines still in our world, shining over the location of the Christ. The star is still there in the hurts that must be healed, the deeds that must be done, the lost that must be reached—in of all the areas that the Christ came to work.

Wise persons embark on the journey. They will not be deterred by its length or difficulty. They will not be deceived by the Herods who call them foolish nor sidetracked by the distractions that offer temporary fulfillment. They will follow the yearning in their hearts until they find the Christ and the meaning and joy that only he can give. Wise men and women, wise young people, wise boys and girls will worship him and give him the only gift they can bring: the gift of their lives.

Day Seven
Simeon, a Man of Anticipation

Now there was a man in Jerusalem whose name was Simeon; this man was righteous and devout, looking forward to the consolation of Israel, and the Holy Spirit rested on him.

—(Luke 2:25)

Sometimes I think we are better at getting ready for some great event than we are at appreciating it and celebrating it once it has arrived. We have a hard time handling fulfillment. We do not always know how to act or what to say. Is it not ironic that we put forth so much time and effort getting ready to observe the birth of our Lord and then, when Christmas comes, we are anxious to turn our attention to other things? Let's not take that approach. Let's not simply give the Christ child a hasty expression of praise and then return unaffected to our regular routines and responsibilities. Let us feel and explore the fulfillment that his arrival brings.

For me, Simeon, the aged man that Mary and Joseph encountered in the temple, represents this perspective on Christmas. Our study of the Christmas narratives in the Gospels would be incomplete if we did not include his prophetic story. Our own observance of Christmas would be incomplete if we did not come to grips with the sense of fulfillment that Simeon expressed.

Forty days after Jesus was born, Mary and Joseph took him from Bethlehem to the temple in Jerusalem "to present him to the Lord." The description of this ritual by Luke, given in such a matter-of-fact way, conveys some interesting insights into the kind of home into which Jesus was born. The timing of the circumcision and presentation of Jesus and the observance of the ceremonial purification for Mary indicate that Joseph and Mary were devout in their piety and adherence to the Jewish law. The fact that they brought "a pair of turtledoves or two young pigeons" as a sacrifice shows that they would be counted among the poor. Had they been better off, they would have brought a year-old lamb. To a humble but deeply religious family our Lord came and grew up.

In the temple a strange thing happened. The parents and the child were not able to come and go with anonymity. They were approached by an elderly man named Simeon who wanted to hold the baby. All parents are thrilled when someone notices their child. I suppose this was especially true for Mary, for she had been isolated for almost six weeks following Jesus' birth. If there was hesitation on her part, her fears were quickly put to rest by the saintly face of Simeon. What followed when Simeon took Jesus into his arms was a highly emotional moment that Mary would remember for as long as she lived.

Cradling the Christ child, Simeon prayed, "Master, now you are dismissing your servant in peace, according to your word; for my eyes have seen your salvation, which you have prepared in the presence of all peoples, a light for revelation to the Gentiles and for glory to your people Israel" (Luke 2:29-31).

For Mary and Joseph, Simeon's prayer was a confirmation of what they had received by angelic announcement. This child was unique! For Simeon the prayer was an expression of fulfillment. He had lived to see the messiah.

Who was this man who gave such a meaningful interpretation to the Christmas story? Like every pious Jew, Simeon believed his own nation to be a chosen people, and he harbored the belief in the anointed one of God who would some day come as deliverer. While most of his countrymen anticipated a military champion, however, in the tradition of King David, who would revive the nation's glory, Simeon and a few others like him, took a different view.

This group had no dreams of violence and power. They were known by many as "the quiet of the land," conceived the "consolation of Israel" as the time when God would send a messiah to comfort the people. No, Simeon and his kind did not plan for battle; they labored in prayer. They did not take part in plots against Rome; they patiently waited for God's deliverance.

Agitators and warriors came and went, but this group preserved the hope of Israel. What a wondrous hope it was! The words of Isaiah were ever in their minds: "Comfort, O comfort my people" (40:1); "The people who walked in darkness have seen a great light" (9:2); "A shoot shall come out from the stump of Jesse" (11:1); "For a child has been born for us; a son is given to us" (9:6). These promises sustained Israel. During exile and control by foreign powers, during famine and hard times, during defeat and tragedy, one hope kept recurring. One day he will come; one day the messiah will come!

Somehow Simeon came to believe that the "consolation of Israel" would become a living reality in his own time. His faith came to rest, not in some far-off future event, but in God's activity in the present. Luke says that through the revelation of the Holy Spirit, Simeon developed the conviction that he would live to see the Lord's Christ, that his hope would find fulfillment.

Hope deferred too long loses its power to sustain us. Loss of hope is a tragic thing in a person's life. We see many persons who give up hope for solving their difficulties, creating a better world, or developing a life of integrity. Consequently, they turn away from Christ to pursue some other key to meaningful life. Notice that Simeon was an old man. He had not given up on prayer, nor the religious institution (he found Christ in the temple); he had not given up hope. Simeon was committed to the promises God had made, long though their realization became. He found fulfillment.

As he returned the baby Jesus to his mother, Simeon said to Mary, "This child is destined for the falling and the rising of many in Israel, and to be a sign that will be opposed" (Luke 2:34). Already a shadow, it seems, had begun to fall across the manger and the life of Jesus. By him many shall fall—how does the fulfillment of God's promises become the cause whereby people shall fall?

The coming of Jesus Christ introduces a new standard by which persons and movements are to be judged. The world has its own standards of judgment. It wants to know of any idea or situation whether or not it has the majority on its side, whether or not it has the favorable opinion of the so-called "best people," whether or not it commands financial support. The world evaluates things by the criteria of public opinion, power, and money.

Christ stands over against that. He places spiritual values above material values. He emphasizes the sacred worth of human personality. He teaches redemption through love, and triumph through sacrifice.

The presence of Christ in the world, with his different value system and his different approach to the meaning of life, constitutes a demand for decision. Those who reject him will fall. Anyone who remains coldly unmoved or actively hostile will have no part in his kingdom. By him also many will rise! Those who accept him will be lifted up.

The Christ child will arouse opposition, Simeon said, and then in a poignant word to Mary, he added, "and a sword will pierce your own soul too" (v. 35). That line hurts, and we would like to delete it from the Christmas story, but it has to remain there. Love for Christ and a close relationship with him will make demands of us. We cannot love him without actually following him, and we cannot follow him without making changes and sacrifice.

The skeptic might wonder what is so fulfilling about a message such as this—a message that speaks of opposition, falling, rising, and pain. How can these things point to fulfillment? As Simeon concluded, through Christ, "the inner thoughts of many will be revealed." Through Christ, hearts are opened to goodness, truth, sharing, and love. Herein is the fulfillment that God has promised and that Jesus Christ has brought. We, therefore, celebrate fulfillment and rejoice in the life that has come to us. We rejoice in the life of the babe of Bethlehem, the life that becomes the model for true human life, the life given and the life sacrificed that we might know real life ourselves.

Notes

[1] Viktor E. Frankl, *Man's Search for Meaning: An Introduction to Logotheraphy* (New York: Pocket Books, 1971).

[2] John Ruskin, Letter xii, 23 December 1871. Cited in *The Interpreter's Bible* (New York: Abingdon Press, 1951) 7:258.

The Enduring
Message of Christmas

From Bedlam to Bethlehem

In those days a decree went out from Emperor Augustus that all the world should be registered. This was the first registration and was taken while Quirinius was governor of Syria. All went to their own towns to be registered. Joseph also went from the town of Nazareth in Galilee, to Judea, to the city of David called Bethlehem, because he was descended from the house and family of David. He went to be registered with Mary, to whom he was engaged and who was expecting a child. While they were there, the time came for her to deliver her child.

–(Luke 2:1-7)

In 1247 Saint Mary of Bethlehem Hospital was established in London. About 200 years later it was converted into a facility for the mentally ill. Instead of being a place of healing and quiet, Saint Mary of Bethlehem became a place of confusion and disorder. In time, the longer name passed from popular usage, and the hospital, then an asylum, came to be called simply Bethlehem. In the English way of clipping syllables in words, most people referred to the place as "Beth-lem" and later as "Bedlam." A new word came into the language: bedlam, a place of uproar and confusion.

Word derivations are fascinating. Is it not interesting that Bethlehem, a word that connotes beauty and life, should become bedlam, a harsh word that speaks of chaos? The transition is virtually a parable about the way we distort the good gifts of God. Obviously, we can see that pattern in our observance of what we call the Christmas season. What should be a time of wonder and joy we have made into an annual exercise of busyness and confusion. As we arrive at the time to celebrate the coming of the Prince of Peace, most people would admit to being frantic, fractured, and fragmented.

Our whole way of living and thinking has come to the point of bedlam. If we look at the problems that occupy our time and attention, we wonder how we have so badly missed the message.

From Bedlam to Bethlehem

How can warring factions in poor countries persist in their hostilities and allow their people to starve en masse? That's bedlam! How can racial prejudice and hatred continue? Bedlam! How can we be so concerned about "people like us" that we virtually write off everyone else? Bedlam! Crime, debt, AIDS, family disintegration, the breakdown of values—you name it—it is a world of bedlam. That we have moved from Bethlehem to bedlam is a pattern of human experience.

Bethlehem calls us back, however. Even amid the noise and confusion of bedlam we hear the summons to Bethlehem. We read again that Joseph and Mary "went from the town of Nazareth in Galilee . . . to the city of David called Bethlehem." Thank God for the invitation to Bethlehem. Not just at Christmas, but at all times the invitation is there, the invitation to go "over to Bethlehem to see this thing that has happened."

Where is Bethlehem? We know about the location of bedlam, but where is Bethlehem? How do you get there? Bethlehem is a town in the hill country of Judah or Judea. It traces its history to the time of Jacob the patriarch. Jacob's beloved wife Rachel died and was buried in Bethlehem. The town was given to Caleb, one of the faithful spies and warriors of the Israelites. It was the home of Boaz and Ruth and the birthplace of David, the shepherd boy who became king.

Literally, Bethlehem means "house of bread." The village was set in a fertile farming area. The grain of Bethlehem was marketed in nearby Jerusalem. Many people ate the bread of this town. As the people of God began to look for deliverance and redemption, and as they began to anticipate spiritual nourishment, Bethlehem became a house of bread in a much broader sense. The God who had raised up David as king, the people thought, would bring forth the branch of David, the messiah, who would feed and satisfy his people. Micah the prophet voiced these hopes: "But you, O Bethlehem of Ephrathah, who are one of the little clans of Judah, from you shall come forth for me one who is to be ruler in Israel" (5:2, 4).

In God's time came the fulfillment! The Christ came in Bethlehem—the Messiah, God in flesh, the ultimate expression of love. Indeed, the house of bread provides the Bread of Life. A place of humility provides greatness. A child provides strength and maturity.

We need to move from bedlam to Bethlehem. Our hearts ache for the journey. Why do the texts we hear at Christmas evoke such strong feelings? Bethlehem calls us, and something deep inside yearns to make the pilgrimage. The trip is not a physical one, however. You probably would not want to go to the physical Bethlehem this week. The place called Bethlehem is more like bedlam. It's a pawn in the ongoing struggles between the Jews and the Arabs. The real Bethlehem, however, the Bethlehem of Christ, is available to all of us and invites all of us.

We move from bedlam to Bethlehem when we hear, believe, and accept the great announcement that our savior has come. We affirm that Jesus Christ initiates and sustains life. We cannot live by bread alone. We need the nourishment of the Bread of Life that issues from the "house of bread." Apart from this nourishment there is only weakness and confusion. But a Savior is born. God has come to be with us. Life has new possibilities. When we hear that word and come to believe it, we are approaching the precincts of Bethlehem.

We move from bedlam to Bethlehem when we live in the peace that the Savior came to bring. Do you remember the song of the angels? Bedlam is chaos; Bethlehem is peace. Measure the peace in your heart, and you know where you are.

A reporter looking for a story went through an inner city ghetto. He found an old man living in a rundown tenement building. Gangs roamed the streets outside, writing graffiti on the walls, destroying mailboxes, and terrorizing the elderly citizens when they tried to go to the store. Behind the tenement, a wrecking ball crashed into a building, and a jackhammer kept pounding the concrete. "How can you stand to live here?" asked the reporter. The old man nodded to a small crucifix on the wall. "He creates a little circle of quiet and peace. Haven't you noticed?" The reporter had not. The story was written and printed. The reporter wrote about the bedlam, but the old man lived in Bethlehem.

We are speaking about a spiritual thing! But it is real—more real than the physical. You move from bedlam to Bethlehem when you allow the God of love and peace into your life, when you give the Christ the central place. Apart from that there is no Bethlehem, only bedlam.

I've thought a great deal about the way the term bedlam grew out of the word Bethlehem. You naturally ask how that could happen. I think now I know. I am indebted to psychiatrist Scott Peck for an idea that I'm still trying to work into my thought system. Peck says that we assume that life is supposed to be easy, simple, and good. Consequently, we seem surprised by illness or express dismay at bad news. We think the good is the norm and the bad is unusual. Peck says that the reverse is true. The bad is the norm. Life is filled with uncertainty and hardship; illness, misfortune, and death are natural processes. What is unusual and worthy of note is the good. Is this not the message of Christmas? Into a world of bedlam, order, peace, strength, and healing have come. That is "good news of great joy." It requires movement and change—a change of heart, a change of residence.

If you visit the Bethlehem that is a physical location adjacent to Jerusalem, you will be taken to the Church of the Nativity. Under the church is a cave where, according to accounts that go back to the second century, Christians have said that Christ was born. It's hard to get a perspective, because the whole area is covered with stone slabs and tapestries, and smoky lamps give off a faint light. A short distance from the grotto of the nativity is another cave. This one was a study used by Saint Jerome, the founder of Latin monasticism, from 384 A.D. until his death in 420. Jerome translated the Old Testament into Latin and established a convent in Bethlehem. Jerome moved to Bethlehem because he wanted to escape the decadence of Rome. He labored in the cave next door to the birthplace of the Christ and said that he constantly received inspiration from his proximity to the holy site.

You and I cannot move physically to Bethlehem, but we can still move to Bethlehem. We can take up our abode with Christ. His peace can be ours. The wonder, the beauty, the goodness—all the blessings of Bethlehem are available to us here in our bedlam.

Christmas Day
Home for Christmas

And she gave birth to her firstborn son and wrapped him in bands of cloth,
and laid him in a manger, because there was no place for them in the inn.
—(Luke 2:7)

The other day on the car radio I heard Perry Como croon, "There's No Place Like Home for the Holidays." A few minutes later came that plaintive song, "I'll Be Home for Christmas." The lyrics of these songs and many other favorites of the season evoke a profound emotional response. At Christmas time almost everyone's thoughts turn toward home. In fact, a survey I saw reveals that Christmas is the one time of year when most people want to be home. It leads birthdays by three to one and the Fourth of July by five to one.

It is tempting to dismiss the connection between home and Christmas as mere sentimentality. We have to admit that past Christmases may not have been as wonderful as we say. When we search memory honestly, we are aware of pain and disappointment as well as fulfillment and joy. To say that we are simply exploiting nostalgia, however, is not a sufficient explanation for the feelings we have. Something deeper is at work. Home and Christmas are closely connected.

I derived a new appreciation of the centrality of home in Christmas through a word study by the biblical scholar Kenneth Bailey. For several years Bailey lived, studied, and taught just outside the city of Bethlehem. Out of his knowledge of the biblical languages and his familiarity with Middle Eastern customs, Bailey gives a unique interpretation to the story of Jesus' birth.

In our usual telling of the story we say that Joseph and Mary made the long journey from Nazareth, where Joseph had a carpentry shop, to Bethlehem, his ancestral home, in order to be registered in the Roman census. While they were in Bethlehem, the time came for the birth of the baby Mary was carrying. Matthew's gospel also has a birth narrative, but it says nothing about the place of the birth. Luke's account gives one line: The child was laid in a manger "because there was no place for them in the inn." From that one note we construct a full story. We imagine Joseph going from one inn to another in the village and reason that finally some innkeeper had sympathy on the young couple and gave them the use of his stable. There, with Mary and Joseph lonely and far from home, the Christ child was born.

Bailey raises interesting questions about that version of the story. He says that the Greek word that is translated "inn" really means "guest room." There is another word for "inn," and if Luke had been speaking of hostelry, he would have used it. The line, according to Bailey, should read: "because there was no place for them in the guest room."

One should understand the floor plan of the typical Middle Eastern house. In such a house, the living room often doubles as a guest room. Overnight visitors or relatives sleep in this room. To the side, on a lower level, if possible, or in a cave, if one is available, is an outer room where the family's animals are kept. You can find houses even today with this kind of arrangement. If the house were to overflow with people, the host would sweep out the stable area and allow guests to sleep there.

We should also remember the place of hospitality in Middle Eastern villages. If you were to go to Israel and get out of the cities into the countryside, people would invite you and your whole tour group into their homes. Mary and Joseph were in Joseph's hometown. They were among kinfolk. It would have been unthinkable for them to seek a room in a public inn.

So, let's tell the story differently, perhaps more accurately. Mary and Joseph came to Bethlehem and sought out Joseph's relatives. Because many other relatives were there as well, there was no place for them in the "guest room." The couple needed privacy anyway, so they were taken to the side of the house and given the stable. If this approach is correct, Jesus therefore was not born away from home and family. He was born with aunts and uncles and cousins and possibly grandparents waiting anxiously to hear his first cry. The extended family was present. Jesus was at home when he came into this world.

I am deeply moved by this thought. It certainly fits our theological understanding of the coming of Christ. Our view is that in the Christ child God has taken up abode with us. The prophets said that God would "tabernacle" with us, specifically that God would pitch a tent and live with us. The angel said to Joseph that the child would be called Immanuel, which means "God with us." Quite simply, we affirm at Christmas that God has made a home with us. There is a certain harmony between this understanding of the Incarnation and the idea that Jesus was born not among strangers but in the bosom of a large family.

The word "home" touches the core of human need. For most people, home means security and acceptance. It means, or it should mean, unconditional love and safety, a place in which one can grow and develop. Home is more than the provision of need, however. It gives identity. From home and family, says sociologist Robert Bellah, we derive a sense of belonging through what he calls a "common narrative." We tell and retell experiences we have shared and cement the bond between ourselves and those whom we love.

At the same time, the actual experience of being at home at Christmas will not likely satisfy our full expectations. We are both burdened and blessed by an essential homesickness for eternity, a homesickness that is satisfied only when we are at home with God who has come to be at home with us, a homesickness that will be filled only when we are at home with others. Consequently, I don't denigrate songs or talk about being home for Christmas. We are responding to a need that goes beyond description, a need that all people have, whether they can remember a happy home or not. We need a place to go, full of acceptance and love.

Arthur Gordon tells a story called "The Homecoming." It is about a salesman names Wilbur Stevens. One day Wilbur came into the office after lunch and jubilantly announced that he had made the biggest sale of his career. He had sold 15,000 electric motors produced by his company to another firm. The commission would be more than his usual year's salary. He told his secretary, "The order will be confirmed in writing by a messenger this afternoon."

Wilbur couldn't work. He kept thinking about how to spend the money he would receive. Immediately, he called a jewelry store and ordered an expensive watch for his wife, then the florist for a dozen roses. Next he thought about buying a new refrigerator, painting the house, getting a new car, putting some funds back for the children's college costs.

Wilbur Stevens couldn't wait to go home. At mid-afternoon he impatiently buzzed his secretary. "That messenger here yet?" he asked. "Not yet, Mr. Stevens," came the reply. At 4:00, 4:30, and 5:00 P.M. came the same question and the same answer. Wilbur began to feel uneasy. After five o'clock he tried to call the buyer to find out what was wrong. The order had not been confirmed; he could not leave the office. "Mr. Cavanaugh has left for the day," Wilbur was told. More waiting, more misery. Why didn't Cavanaugh call? Had he forgotten to send the confirmation? Wilbur called home to say he would be late.

Wilbur tried to locate his buyer. He remembered that Cavanaugh had said he would be at the athletic club in the evening. Wilbur called the club. When he took the phone, Cavanaugh said, "Look, Wilbur, I'm sorry. This is terrible. It seems that my boss' son-in-law sells for Monarch Motors. When I told him I bought from you, he hit the ceiling. So I placed the order with Monarch."

Wilbur did not arrive home until after 11:00 P.M. He had left the watch in his office drawer. There was nothing to do with the flowers but take them home. So many hopes, so many expectations, such a deep feeling of failure! But Wilbur was home! He took one flower and went to the bedroom. His wife Barbara was still awake. "This is for you," he said. "Why, Will, what a surprise! What's it for?" Wilbur could only say, "It's for you." Barbara replied, "This is a wonderful ending to a long day! How did it go for you?" Wilbur Stevens thought of the wealth that got away. But he felt the love of home, the acceptance of his family, and he said, "It was fine. It was a very useful day."

God has made a home with us. God has given us a place to go regardless of what we have done or failed to do. When we understand the true value of things, we let our hearts drift toward home.

The Day after Christmas
Returning from Bethlehem

When the angels had left them and gone into heaven, the shepherds said to one another, "Let us go over to Bethlehem and see this thing that has taken place, which the Lord has made known to us." So they went with haste and found Mary and Joseph, and the child lying in a manger. When they saw this, they made known what had been told them about this child; and all who heard it were amazed at what the shepherds told them. But Mary treasured all these words and pondered them in her heart. The shepherds returned, glorifying and praising God for all they had heard and seen, as it had been told them.

—(Luke 2:15-20)

I have often heard it said that "nothing is quite so over as Christmas on December 26." Many persons, I suppose—weary with shopping, decorating, and hurrying about—are delighted that it is. It's rather ironic that after such a lengthy period of preparation and anticipation, we are so ready to let the season pass.

Moving beyond the busyness of Christmas and back into a normal routine can be a welcome relief. But, if in putting away our decorations we also put aside the spirit of celebration we have felt, if in storing the creche for another year we also put away the Christ, if in placing our gifts among our other possessions we forget the love of those who have given, we suffer an unfortunate loss.

Moving beyond Christmas does not mean that something has ended, but rather that we have added a new dimension to life. The church leaders who began the formation of the Christian calendar placed Advent and Christmastide at the beginning of the Christian year. For them the season represented a perpetual new start. Our observance of the birth of Jesus Christ rejoices in the past, present, and future. We proclaim the salvation of God promised in the past, realized in the present, and completed in the future. In that sense, Christmas is never really over.

From Bedlam to Bethlehem

Luke the physician, ever the careful storyteller, does not terminate his account of the first Christmas with the abruptness with which so many are willing to leave Christmas today. He lingers at the manger, describing not only the beauty and glory of the scene but also the effect of the Christ child on those first witnesses.

Luke, as you know, gives the shepherds a prominent place in the Christmas story. To these simple, hard-working men came the announcement that the Savior, Messiah, Immanuel!, had been born. Before their bewildered eyes the angelic chorus sang, "Glory to God in the highest heaven, and on earth peace among those whom he favors!" When the angels had gone away, the shepherds said to one another, "Let us go now to Bethlehem and see this thing that has taken place." The narrative tells of their hasty search for the child, their reverent adoration, and their eagerness to share with others what they had witnessed.

Luke rounds off his story by going beyond Christmas. He adds, "The shepherds returned." In my mind's eye, I can see them at daybreak (on 26 December, if you will), going back to the hillside, back to their work. The return from Bethlehem was far different from the journey into town. The breathless anticipation was gone. The keen sense of expectancy had given way to a return to the ordinary and the commonplace.

The road back is like that. We know the feeling. We know the excitement of leaving for a trip or vacation. The anticipation is part of the pleasure; the travel to our destination becomes an adventure. The time comes when we have to return home, though. All great experiences have a road back. Although "there is no place like home," we have a reluctance to resume that which is routine. We feel a letdown.

The atmosphere on the days after Christmas is far different from that on the days before. During Advent we asked, what will Christmas mean? Now we ask, what has it meant? Now we turn our attention from the wonder of the child in the manger to the influence of the living Christ in our lives. I'm not one to rush the season; the child in me would never hasten the end of Christmas. Just as we go into Bethlehem, though, we have to return to the hillside.

142

The Day after Christmas Returning from Bethlehem

What are we taking back with us? What will our moments of worship and the feelings we have experienced leave with us that will enhance our process of becoming new persons? Thankfully, Luke said more about the shepherds than that they simply returned. They went back, "Glorifying and praising God for all they had heard and seen." They took back with them an experience that would leave them forever transformed. Life would no longer be as it was.

Years later as the aged apostle John penned what we call his first epistle, he described an awareness that the unlettered shepherds might have felt but could not express. He spoke of hearing, seeing, and touching "that which was from the beginning," "the eternal life that was with the Father," "and was revealed to us" (1:1-4). The shepherds could not attach theological significance to what they saw, but they recognized without hesitation that God had done something wonderful among them. They accepted God's work, and therefore received everlasting joy.

Personal experience touches us in a way that argument and speculation never can. We should not leave Christmas without a renewal of our experience of God's gift in Jesus Christ, without being reminded that "God is with us," without simply and humbly "feeling" again that love God has shown in giving his son.

Not only did the shepherds take back with them a recognition of what God had done, but also they walked the road back with the afterglow of a whole-hearted response to the child. They had worshiped the Christ with sincere devotion and adoration. What happened to them later we are not told. Perhaps some of these men lived to see the ministry of Jesus, witness his works, and hear his words.

Unfortunately, we do not know more about the shepherds and how their late night trip to Bethlehem influenced their lives. Nevertheless, they left us an example of the proper response to the child. They gave him their spontaneous love. Isn't that our appropriate response? We truly observe Christmas only when we allow it to deepen our devotion to Christ. Christmas is not just a time for the delight of discovery; it is a time for growth as well.

The shepherds also took back with them a sense of the new possibilities the Christ child represented. They could not keep silent about what they had experienced. They "made known what had been told them about this child." No doubt they "made known" much more, for God had invaded their mundane existence.

Christmas reminds us of our responsibility not just to adore the Christ child, but to serve him. How tragic it would be for Christmas to pass without our feeling anew that call. Many people, however, move beyond Christmas and go back to their usual ruts. If God has indeed entered our lives, if God has really come "unto us," how can we act as though nothing has happened? We have a life to live for Christ and a word to spread about him. We have bowed before the child, and in doing so we accept all that he represents. We accept his love, but more than that, we accept his challenge and command.

The child did not remain an infant. He moved beyond Bethlehem to become a man who brought to realization all that Christmas represents. The child became a man who said: "Follow me" (Mark 1:17); "Go . . . do not sin again" (John 8:11); "You cannot serve God and wealth" (Matt 6:24); "Blessed are those who are persecuted for righteousness' sake" (Matt 5:10).

The return from Bethlehem means that we move from the infancy of Christ to his maturity and we allow our infant faith to grow and develop. So much depends on our response and the responsibility we assume for God's gift. At Christmastime, Christ has come to us again; let us come to him, receive the divine gift of God, and allow him to be our eternal companion.